09-BUB-659

AP® U.S. GOVERNMENT AND POLITICS
CRASH COURSE®

By Larry Krieger

Research & Education Association
Visit our website at: www.rea.com

Research & Education Association
61 Ethel Road West
Piscataway, New Jersey 08854
E-mail: info@rea.com

AP® U.S. GOVERNMENT AND POLITICS CRASH COURSE®

Published 2015

Printed in the United States of America

Library of Congress Control Number 2009940570

ISBN-13: 978-0-7386-0809-9
ISBN-10: 0-7386-0809-2

Crash Course® and REA® are registered trademarks of
Research & Education Association, Inc.

AP U.S. GOVERNMENT AND POLITICS CRASH COURSE TABLE OF CONTENTS

PART I: **Introduction**

PART II: **Key Content Review**

PART III: Key Themes and Facts

PART IV: Test-Taking Strategies

Online Practice Exam .... *www.rea.com/studycenter*

ABOUT THIS BOOK

REA's *AP U.S. Government and Politics Crash Course* is the first book of its kind for the last-minute studier or any AP student who wants a quick refresher on the course. The *Crash Course* is based upon a careful analysis of the AP U.S. Government and Politics Course Description outline and actual AP test questions.

Written by an expert who has studied the AP U.S. Government and Politics exam content, our easy-to-read format gives students a crash course in the major ideas and events in U.S. government and politics. The targeted review chapters prepare students for the exam by focusing on the important topics tested on the AP U.S. Government and Politics exam.

Unlike other test preps, REA's *AP U.S. Government and Politics Crash Course* gives you a review specifically focused on what you really need to study in order to ace the exam. The review chapters offer you a concise way to learn all the important facts, terms, and key themes before the exam.

The introduction discusses the keys for success and shows you strategies to help you build your overall point score. It also gives you a list of Key Terms that you absolutely, positively have to know. Parts Two and Three are composed of chapters offering content and factual reviews. Each chapter presents the essential information you need to know about U.S. Government and Politics.

Part Four focuses exclusively on the format of the AP U.S. Government and Politics exam. Each chapter in this section explains specific strategies for the multiple-choice questions and the free-response essays.

No matter how or when you prepare for the AP U.S. Government and Politics exam, REA's *Crash Course* will show you how to study efficiently and strategically, so you can boost your score!

To check your test readiness for the AP U.S. Government and Politics exam, either before or after studying this *Crash Course*, take REA's **FREE online practice exam**. To access your practice exam, visit the online REA Study Center at *www.rea.com/studycenter* and follow the on-screen instructions. This true-to-format test features automatic scoring, detailed explanations of all answers, and diagnostic score reporting that will help you identify your strengths and weaknesses so you'll be ready on exam day!

Good luck on your AP U.S. Government and Politics exam!

ABOUT OUR AUTHOR

Larry Krieger earned his B.A. and M.A.T. from the University of North Carolina at Chapel Hill and his M.A. from Wake Forest University. In a career spanning more than 35 years, Mr. Krieger has taught a variety of AP subjects including American History, World History, European History, American Government, and Art History. His popular courses were renowned for their energetic presentations, commitment to scholarship, and helping students achieve high AP exam scores. All of Mr. Krieger's students scored above a 3, with most students scoring a 4 or a 5. In 2004 and 2005, the College Board recognized Mr. Krieger as one of the nation's foremost AP teachers.

Mr. Krieger's success has extended far beyond the classroom. He is the author of several widely used American History and World History textbooks, along with REA's AP Art History test preparation guide. In addition, he has spoken at numerous Social Studies conferences and conducts SAT and AP workshops around the country. His new venture, the *AP Crash Courses*, is an innovative new series of test preparation books from REA that will help students strategically and effectively prepare for their AP exams.

ACKNOWLEDGMENTS

In addition to our author, we would like to thank Larry B. Kling, Vice President, Editorial, for his overall guidance, which brought this publication to completion; Pam Weston, Vice President, Publishing, for setting the quality standards for production integrity and managing the publication to completion; Diane Goldschmidt, Senior Editor, for editorial project management; Alice Leonard, Senior Editor, for preflight editorial review; Rachel DiMatteo, Graphic Artist, for page design; and Weymouth Design for designing our cover.

We would also like to extend special thanks to Marianne L'Abbate for copyediting, Ellen Gong for proofreading, and Kathy Caratozzolo of Caragraphics for typesetting this edition.

PART I:

INTRODUCTION

Seven Keys for Success on the AP U.S. Government and Politics Exam

AP U.S. Government and Politics textbooks are very thick and contain hundreds of terms, acts of Congress, and Supreme Court decisions. If all of these facts had an equal chance of appearing on your Advanced Placement U.S. Government and Politics exam, studying would be a nightmare. Where would you begin? What would you emphasize? As you prepare for this exam, is there any information you can safely omit? Or must you study everything?

1. **Understanding the AP U.S. Government and Politics Scale**

   Many students believe they must make close to a perfect score to receive a 5. Nothing could be further from the truth. Each AP U.S. Government and Politics exam contains a total of 120 points—60 from the multiple-choice and 60 from the free-response questions. Here is the typical score range from released exams:

Score Range	AP Grade	Minimum Percent Right
90–120	5	75 percent
75–89	4	62 percent
60–74	3	50 percent
36–59	2	30 percent
0–35	1	29 percent

This chart is not a misprint. As is clearly shown, you can usually achieve a 5 by correctly answering just 75 percent of the questions, a 4 by correctly answering just 62 percent of the questions, and a 3 by correctly answering just 50 percent of the questions.

2. Understanding the AP U.S. Government and Politics Curriculum Outline

Many students believe that members of the AP U.S. Government and Politics exam development committee have the freedom to write any question they wish. This widespread belief is not true. AP U.S. Government and Politics test writers use a detailed curriculum outline that tells them the topics that can be tested. The curriculum outline is freely available in the *AP U.S. Government and Politics Course Description Booklet*. Here are the six major topics and the percentage of multiple-choice questions devoted to each topic.

The Constitution and Federalism	5–15 percent
Political Beliefs, Public Opinion and Voting	10–20 percent
Political Parties, Interest Groups, and Mass Media	10–20 percent
The Three Branches of the Federal Government and the Bureaucracy	35–45 percent
Public Policy and the Budget	5–15 percent
Civil Liberties and Civil Rights	5–15 percent

3. Understanding the Importance of the Released Exams and the AP Central Collection of Free-Response Questions

The College Board has released AP U.S. Government and Politics exams for the years 1989, 1994, 1999, 2002, and 2009. In addition, they provided an online exam for all teachers who participated in the AP course audit. Taken together, these six exams contain 360 released multiple-choice questions. In addition, the College Board's AP Central website contains a full discussion of all the free-response questions asked from 1999 to the present.

Your *Crash Course* book is based upon a careful analysis of all the released multiple-choice and free-response questions. These questions can be used to understand the priorities and patterns of the AP U.S. Government and Politics test writers. It is important to understand that the test writers' top priority is to write an exam that is a valid and reliable measure of a defined body of knowledge. As a result, test questions cluster around very predictable and often-repeated topics.

4. Understanding the Importance of Key Topics

AP U.S. Government and Politics topics are not all covered equally. Some topics are far more important than others. A detailed analysis of the released multiple-choice and free-response questions reveals the following three key clusters of questions:

> ‣ Congress and the Presidency: *These are by far the two most important topics tested on the AP U.S. Government and Politics exam. Taken together they generate almost 33 percent of the multiple-choice questions and 40 percent of all free-response questions. It is important to note that every exam since 1999 has had at least one free-response question devoted to Congress and/or the President.*

> ‣ The Supreme Court, Civil Liberties, and Civil Rights: *These three topics form a very cohesive unit. Taken together, they generate 20 percent of all multiple-choice questions and 15 percent of all free-response questions. Supreme Court cases play a very important role in this topical package. Contrary to popular belief, it is not necessary to memorize lengthy lists of Supreme Court cases. There are actually only about 30 cases you absolutely, positively have to know. Chapter 17 provides a concise summary of the key rulings in each of these key cases.*

> ‣ The Top Twenty Topics: *AP U.S. Government and Politics test writers focus a great deal of attention on a relatively small number of key terms and political processes. Chapter 19 provides a concise discussion of the top twenty topics. Taken together, these topics generate almost 33 percent of all multiple-choice questions and 25 percent of all free-response questions.*

5. Understanding the Overlap Between the Multiple-Choice Questions and the Free-Response Questions

Both the multiple-choice questions and the free-response questions are taken from the Curriculum Outline in the Course Description Booklet. As a result, studying for the multiple-choice questions is tantamount to studying for the free-response questions. Most students fail to grasp the significance of this point. Since the multiple-choice questions are highly predictable, so are the free-response questions.

For example, incumbency, federalism, and the selection of Supreme Court justices have each generated a significant number of multiple-choice questions and at least one free-response question.

6. Using Your Crash Course Book to Build a Winning Coalition of Points

This *Crash Course* book is based upon a careful analysis of the Course Description topical outline and the released questions. Chapter 2 contains key terms that you absolutely, positively have to know. Chapters 3–16 provide you with a detailed discussion of each content area covered on the AP U.S. Government and Politics exam. Chapters 17–19 provide you with concise lists of key Supreme Court cases, key acts of Congress, and 20 key topics. And finally, Chapters 20 and 21 discuss test-taking strategies for the multiple-choice and free-response questions.

If you have the time, review the entire book. This is desirable, but not mandatory. The chapters can be studied in any order. Each chapter provides you with a digest of key information that is repeatedly tested. Unlike most review books, the digests are not meant to be exhaustive. Instead, they are meant to focus your attention on the vital material you must study.

Focus your attention on studying a group of topics that will generate a winning coalition of the points you need to score a 4 or 5. Key terms, Congress, the presidency, and Supreme Court cases are the essential building blocks of any successful coalition of points.

7. Using Materials to Supplement Your *Crash Course*

This *Crash Course* contains everything you need to know to score a 4 or 5 on your exam, but an exceptional student like yourself will want to make use of everything that can help. The College Board's website, *www.apcentral.collegeboard.org*, has a wealth of useful information, including past essay questions and sample student essays. In addition, REA's *AP U.S. Government and Politics All Access* Book + Web + Mobile study system further enhances your exam preparation by offering a comprehensive review book plus a suite of online assessments (chapter quizzes, mini-tests, a full-length practice test, and e-flashcards) all designed to pinpoint your strengths and weaknesses and help focus your study for the exam.

Key Terms

I. THE CONSTITUTION AND FEDERALISM

1. MAJORITY RULE

   A fundamental democratic principle requiring that the majority's view be respected. Nonetheless, the Constitution originally contained a number of provisions designed to limit majority rule, including the electoral college, life tenure for Supreme Court justices, and the selection of senators by state legislators.

2. CHECKS AND BALANCES

   System in which each branch of government can limit the power of the other two branches. For example, the Senate has the power to approve or reject presidential appointments to the Supreme Court.

3. UNITARY SYSTEM

   System of government in which all power is invested in a central government.

4. FEDERALISM

   A system of government in which power is divided by a written constitution between a central government and regional governments. As a result, two or more levels of government have formal authority over the same geographic area and people.

5. EXPRESSED POWERS

   Powers specifically granted to the federal government by the Constitution. For example, the Constitution gives Congress the power to coin money, impose taxes, and regulate interstate commerce. Expressed powers are also called enumerated powers.

6. IMPLIED POWERS

   Powers of the federal government that go beyond those enumerated in the Constitution. Implied powers are derived from the elastic or necessary and proper clause.

7. RESERVED POWERS

   Powers not specifically granted to the national government or denied to the states. Reserved powers are held by the states through the Tenth Amendment.

8. COOPERATIVE FEDERALISM

   Situations in which the national and state governments work together to complete projects. Also called fiscal federalism.

9. CATEGORICAL GRANT

   Funds provided for a specific and clearly defined purpose.

10. BLOCK GRANT

    Funds granted to the states for a broadly defined purpose. Because block grants shift resources from the federal government to the states, they contribute to the growing number of state and local government employees.

11. MANDATES

    Rules telling states what they must do to comply with federal guidelines. Unfunded mandates require state and local governments to provide services or comply with regulations without the provision of funds.

12. DEVOLUTION

    A movement to transfer the responsibilities of governing from the federal government to state and local governments.

 ## POLITICAL BELIEFS, PUBLIC OPINION, AND VOTING

13. POLITICAL CULTURE

    A set of widely shared political beliefs and values. America's political culture is characterized by strong support for individual liberty, political equality, legal equality, the rule of law, and limited government.

14. POLITICAL SOCIALIZATION

    The process by which political values are formed and passed from one generation to the next. The family is the most important agent of political socialization.

15. PUBLIC OPINION

    Attitudes about institutions, leaders, political issues, and events.

16. POLITICAL IDEOLOGY

    A cohesive set of beliefs about politics, public policy, and the role of government.

17. POLITICAL EFFICACY

    The belief that one's political participation makes a difference.

18. SPLIT-TICKET VOTING

    Voting for candidates of different parties for different offices in the same election. Recent elections have witnessed a significant increase in split-ticket voting as the number of voters who identify themselves as independents increases.

III. POLITICAL PARTIES, INTEREST GROUPS, AND MASS MEDIA

19. POLITICAL PARTY

    A group of citizens who organize to win elections, hold public offices, operate governments and determine public policy.

20. PLURALITY ELECTION

    The winning candidate is the person who receives more votes than anyone else, but less than half the total.

21. SINGLE-MEMBER DISTRICT

    An electoral district from which one person is chosen by the voters for each elected office. This type of electoral system typically leads to legislatures dominated by two political parties.

22. PARTY ERA

    An historical period dominated by one political party.

23. CRITICAL ELECTION

    An election when significant groups of voters change their traditional patterns of party loyalty.

24. PARTY REALIGNMENT

    The majority party is displaced by the minority party, thus ushering in a new party era. For example, in 1932, Franklin Delano Roosevelt (FDR) led the New Deal coalition of blue-collar workers, racial minorities, Southerners, and farm laborers to a sweeping electoral victory.

25. DIVIDED GOVERNMENT

A government in which one party controls the presidency while another party controls Congress. The pattern of divided government has dominated U.S. politics since the early 1970s.

26. INTEREST GROUP

An organization of people whose members share views on specific interests and attempt to influence public policy to their benefit. Unlike political parties, interest groups do not elect people to office.

27. POLITICAL ACTION COMMITTEE (PAC)

A committee formed by business, labor, or other interest groups to raise money and make contributions to the campaigns of political candidates whom they support.

28. FREE RIDERS

People who benefit from an interest group without making any contributions. Labor unions and public interest groups often have a free-rider problem because people can benefit from the group's activities without joining.

29. POWER ELITE THEORY

The theory that a small number of very wealthy individuals, powerful corporate interest groups, and large financial institutions dominate key policy areas.

30. PLURALIST THEORY

The theory that many interest groups compete for power in a large number of policy areas.

31. HYPERPLURALIST THEORY

The theory that government policy is weakened and often contradictory because there are so many competing interest groups.

32. MASS MEDIA

Means of communication such as newspapers, radio, television, and the Internet that can reach large, widely dispersed audiences.

33. LINKAGE INSTITUTIONS

    Institutions that connect citizens to government. The mass media, interest groups, and political parties are the three main linkage institutions.

34. HORSE-RACE JOURNALISM

    The tendency of the media to cover campaigns by emphasizing how candidates stand in the polls instead of where they stand on the issues.

 ## IV. CONGRESS

35. CONGRESSIONAL REDISTRICTING

    The reallocation of the number of representatives each state has in the House of Representatives.

36. GERRYMANDERING

    The legislative process by which the majority party in each state legislature redraws congressional districts to ensure the maximum number of seats for its candidates.

37. INCUMBENT

    An officeholder who is seeking reelection. Incumbency is the single most important factor in determining the outcome of congressional elections.

38. FRANKING PRIVILEGE

    The right of members of Congress to mail newsletters to their constituents at the government's expense.

39. STANDING COMMITTEES

    Permanent subject-matter congressional committees that handle legislation and oversee the bureaucracy.

40. CONFERENCE COMMITTEES

    Temporary bodies that are formed to resolve differences between House and Senate versions of a bill.

41. HOUSE RULES COMMITTEE

    The House Rules Committee sets the guidelines for floor debate. It gives each bill a rule that places the bill on the legislative calendar, limits time for debate, and determines the type of amendments that will be allowed.

42. HOUSE WAYS AND MEANS COMMITTEE

House committee that handles tax bills.

43. SENIORITY

Unwritten rule in both houses of Congress reserving committee chairs to members of the committee with the longest records of continuous service.

44. FILIBUSTER

A way of delaying or preventing action on a bill by using long speeches and unlimited debate to "talk a bill to death."

45. CLOTURE

A Senate motion to end a filibuster. Cloture requires a three-fifths vote.

46. LOGROLLING

Tactic of mutual aid and vote trading among legislators.

47. OVERSIGHT

Congressional review of the activities of an executive agency, department, or office.

48. DELEGATE ROLE OF REPRESENTATION

When members of Congress cast votes based on the wishes of their constituents.

V. PRESIDENTIAL ELECTIONS, THE PRESIDENCY, AND THE BUREAUCRACY

49. CLOSED PRIMARY

A primary in which voters are required to identify a party preference before the election and are not allowed to split their ticket.

50. FRONTLOADING

The recent pattern of states holding primaries early in order to maximize their media attention and political influence. Three-fourths of the presidential primaries are now held between February and mid-March.

51. SOFT MONEY

Contributions to political parties for party-building activities. Soft money contributions are used to circumvent limits on hard money.

52. 527 GROUP

    A tax-exempt organization created to influence the political process; 527 groups are not regulated by the Federal Election Commission because they do not coordinate their activities with a candidate or party.

53. VETO

    The president's constitutional power to reject a bill passed by Congress. Congress may override the veto with a two-thirds vote in each chamber.

54. LINE-ITEM VETO

    The power to veto specific dollar amounts or line items from major congressional spending bills. The Supreme Court struck down the line-item veto as an unconstitutional expansion of the president's veto power.

55. EXECUTIVE AGREEMENT

    A pact between the president and a head of a foreign state. Executive agreements do not have to be approved by the Senate. However, unlike treaties, executive agreements are not part of U.S. law and are not binding on future presidents.

56. EXECUTIVE PRIVILEGE

    The president's power to refuse to disclose confidential information. In *United States v. Nixon* (1974), the Supreme Court ruled that there is no constitutional guarantee of unqualified executive privilege.

57. LAME-DUCK PERIOD

    The period of time in which the president's term is about to come to an end. Presidents typically have less influence during a lame-duck period.

58. BUREAUCRACY

    A large, complex organization of appointed officials.

59. EXECUTIVE ORDER

    A directive, order, or regulation issued by the president. Executive orders are based on constitutional or statutory authority and have the force of law.

60. IRON TRIANGLE

    An alliance among an administrative agency, an interest group, and a congressional committee. Each member of the iron triangle provides key services, information, or policy for the others.

61. ISSUE NETWORK

A network that includes policy experts, media pundits, congressional staff members, and interest groups who regularly debate an issue.

62. POLICY AGENDA

A set of issues and problems that policy makers consider important. The mass media play an important role in influencing the issues which receive public attention.

VI. THE SUPREME COURT

63. APPELLATE JURISDICTION

The authority of a court to hear an appeal from a lower court.

64. SENATORIAL COURTESY

An unwritten tradition whereby the Senate will not confirm nominations for lower court positions that are opposed by a senator of the president's own party from the state in which the nominee is to serve.

65. WRIT OF *CERTIORARI*

An order by the Supreme Court directing a lower court to send up the record in a given case for its review.

66. RULE OF FOUR

The Supreme Court will hear a case if four justices agree to do so.

67. SOLICITOR GENERAL

The solicitor general is responsible for handling all appeals on behalf of the United States government to the Supreme Court.

68. *AMICUS CURIAE* BRIEF

A friend of the court brief filed by an interest group or interested party to influence a Supreme Court decision.

69. *STARE DECISIS*

Stare decisis is a Latin phrase meaning "let the decision stand." The vast majority of Supreme Court decisions are based on precedents established in earlier cases.

70. JUDICIAL RESTRAINT

Philosophy that the Supreme Court should use precedent and the Framers' original intent to decide cases.

71. JUDICIAL ACTIVISM

Philosophy that the Supreme Court must correct injustices when other branches of government or the states refuse to do so.

VII. THE FEDERAL BUDGET

72. MONETARY POLICY

Monetary policy involves regulating the money supply, controlling inflation, and adjusting interest rates. Monetary policy is controlled by the Federal Reserve Board.

73. FISCAL POLICY

Raising and lowering taxes and government spending programs. Fiscal policy is controlled by the executive and legislative branches.

74. ENTITLEMENT PROGRAM

A government-sponsored program that provides mandated benefits to those who meet eligibility requirements. Social Security and Medicare are the government's largest entitlement programs.

75. OFFICE OF MANAGEMENT AND BUDGET (OMB)

The OMB is responsible for preparing the budget that the president submits to Congress.

VIII. CIVIL LIBERTIES AND CIVIL RIGHTS

76. CIVIL LIBERTIES

Legal and constitutional rights that protect individuals from arbitrary acts of government. Civil liberties include freedom of speech and guarantees of a fair trial.

77. CIVIL RIGHTS

Policies designed to protect people against arbitrary or discriminatory treatment by government officials or individuals. Civil rights include laws prohibiting racial and gender discrimination.

78. SELECTIVE INCORPORATION

The case-by-case process by which liberties listed in the Bill of Rights have been applied to the states using the Due Process Clause of the Fourteenth Amendment.

79. **ESTABLISHMENT CLAUSE**

    A provision of the First Amendment that prohibits Congress from establishing an official government-sponsored religion.

80. **FREE EXERCISE CLAUSE**

    A provision of the First Amendment that guarantees each person the right to believe what he or she wants. However, a religion cannot make an act legal that would otherwise be illegal.

81. **CLEAR AND PRESENT DANGER TEST**

    Judicial interpretation of the First Amendment that government may not ban speech unless it poses an imminent threat to society.

82. **WRIT OF HABEAS CORPUS**

    A court order directing that a prisoner be brought before a court and that the court officers show cause why the prisoner should not be released.

83. **BILL OF ATTAINDER**

    A legislative act that provides for the punishment of a person without a court trial.

84. **EX POST FACTO LAW**

    A law applied to an act committed before the law was enacted.

85. **EXCLUSIONARY RULE**

    Supreme Court guideline that prohibits evidence obtained by illegal searches or seizures from being admitted in court.

86. **MIRANDA WARNINGS**

    Warnings that police must read to suspects prior to questioning that advises them of their rights.

87. **STRICT SCRUTINY**

    Supreme Court rule that classification by race and ethnic background is inherently suspect and must be justified by a "compelling public interest."

88. **AFFIRMATIVE ACTION**

    A policy requiring federal agencies, universities, and most employers to take positive steps to remedy the effects of past discrimination.

PART II:

KEY CONTENT REVIEW

The Constitution

I. INTELLECTUAL ORIGINS OF THE CONSTITUTION

A. THE ENLIGHTENMENT

1. The Framers of the Constitution lived in a period of intellectual ferment known as the Enlightenment.
2. European political thinkers and writers challenged traditional views of the relationship between the people and their government.
3. Enlightened ideas took root in the American colonies, where they became the dominant philosophical and political views of the time. Leaders such as Benjamin Franklin, Thomas Jefferson, and James Madison used Enlightened ideas to justify their opposition to the British government.

B. KEY ENLIGHTENED IDEAS

1. Reason
   ▸ *Reason meant the absence of intolerance, bigotry, and superstition.*
   ▸ *Reason could be used to solve social problems and improve society.*
2. Natural laws
   ▸ *Natural laws regulate human society.*
   ▸ *These natural laws can be discovered by human reason.*
3. Progress
   ▸ *Social progress is possible.*
   ▸ *The discovery of laws of government would improve society and make progress inevitable.*

4. Liberty
   ‣ *Europeans lived in societies governed by absolute monarchs who restricted speech, religion, and trade. Enlightened writers wanted to remove these limitations on human liberty.*
   ‣ *Enlightened thinkers believed that intellectual freedom was a natural right. Progress required freedom of expression.*

5. Toleration
   ‣ *Enlightened thinkers opposed superstition, intolerance, and bigotry.*
   ‣ *They advocated full religious tolerance.*

C. KEY POLITICAL WRITERS

1. John Locke (1632–1704)
   ‣ *Locke argued that people are born with "natural rights" that include "life, liberty, and property."*
   ‣ *People form governments to preserve their natural rights. Government is therefore based on the consent of the governed.*
   ‣ *Government is a contract in which rulers promise to protect the people's natural rights.*
   ‣ *If rulers betray the social contract, the people have a right to replace them.*

2. Charles de Montesquieu (1689–1755)
   ‣ *In his* Spirit of the Laws, *Montesquieu concluded that the ideal government separated powers among legislative, executive, and judicial branches.*
   ‣ *This system of divided authority would protect the rights of individuals by preventing one branch of government from gaining unrestricted control over the entire society.*

3. Jean-Jacques Rousseau (1712–1778)
   ‣ *In his* Social Contract, *Rousseau argued that the sovereign power in a state does not lie in a ruler. Instead, it resides in the general will of the community as a whole.*
   ‣ *Rulers are the servants of the community. If they fail to carry out the people's will, they should be removed.*

II. THE ARTICLES OF CONFEDERATION

A. "A FIRM LEAGUE OF FRIENDSHIP"

1. The United States began as a confederation under the Articles of Confederation.
2. The Articles of Confederation established "a firm league of friendship" with a weak national government. Each state retained "its sovereignty, freedom, and independence."
3. The Articles created a unicameral Congress in which each state had one vote.
4. The Articles did not establish executive or judicial branches. Instead, congressional committees handled these functions.

B. FLAWS IN THE ARTICLES OF CONFEDERATION

1. The writers of the Articles of Confederation were reluctant to give the new government powers they had just denied to Parliament.
2. Congress lacked the power to levy taxes. It had to ask the states for revenue.
3. The government lacked both executive and judicial authority. Congress had no means of enforcing its will.
4. Congress did not have the power to regulate or promote commerce among the states.
5. Amendments required a unanimous vote of all 13 states.

C. SHAYS'S REBELLION

1. Frustrated Massachusetts farmers were losing their land because they could not pay debts in hard currency.
2. The farmers demanded an end to foreclosures, relief from oppressively high taxation, and increased circulation of paper money.
3. Led by Daniel Shays, rebellious farmers forced several judges to close their courts.
4. Shays's Rebellion helped convince key leaders that the Articles of Confederation were too weak and that the United States needed a stronger central government that could maintain order, protect property, and promote commerce.

THE FRAMERS

A. "AN ASSEMBLY OF DEMI-GODS"

1. Twelve of the 13 states sent delegations to Philadelphia. The debtors and small farmers who controlled the Rhode Island legislature opposed a stronger central government and refused to send a delegation.

2. Although the state legislatures selected 74 delegates, only 55 actually attended the convention.

3. The delegates included 7 former or current governors, 33 lawyers, 34 college graduates, and 8 signers of the Declaration of Independence.

4. Thomas Jefferson (who was an American minister to France) later called the delegates "an assembly of demi-gods." Success, however, was not inevitable. James Madison recognized that the delegates faced a daunting challenge. He later wrote that "[t]he necessity of gaining the concurrence of the convention in some system that will answer the purpose, the subsequent approbation of Congress, and the final sanction of the states presents a series of chances which would inspire despair in any case where the alternative was less formidable."

B. SHARED IDEAS

1. Human nature
   - ▸ *The delegates believed that people were self-centered and selfish.*
   - ▸ *Franklin underscored this cynical view of human nature when he said, "There are two passions which have a powerful influence on the affairs of men: the love of power and the love of money."*

2. Political conflict
   - ▸ *The unequal distribution of property is the primary source of political conflict. It inevitably creates rival factions.*
   - ▸ *Society is divided into the propertyless majority and the wealthy few.*
   - ▸ *Neither faction could be trusted and therefore both had to be checked.*

3. Purpose of government
   ▸ *The Framers agreed with John Locke that "[t]he preservation of property is the end of government."*
   ▸ *Both the rebellious farmers in Massachusetts and the radical debtors in Rhode Island alarmed the Framers. They feared the threat of "excessive democracy" posed by unruly state governments.*

4. Nature of government
   ▸ *The Framers agreed with Montesquieu that government should be limited and that power should be divided into separate legislative, executive, and judicial branches.*
   ▸ *The Framers supported a limited government with specific powers and a carefully designed set of checks and balances.*

 IV. THE CONSTITUTIONAL CONVENTION: COMPROMISE AND CONSENSUS

A. A MOMENTOUS DECISION

1. Congress called the Philadelphia Convention "for the sole and express purpose" of revising the Articles of Confederation.
2. Less than a week after the Convention opened, the delegates voted to abandon the Articles of Confederation and create a national government with significantly increased power.

B. THE CONNECTICUT (GREAT) COMPROMISE

1. The Virginia Plan
   ▸ *Called for a bicameral legislature.*
   ▸ *Called for representation based on each state's population.*
2. The New Jersey Plan
   ▸ *Called for a unicameral legislature.*
   ▸ *Called for equal representation regardless of a state's population.*
   ▸ *Small state delegates threatened to leave the Convention. Gunner Bedford of Delaware spoke for the small state delegates when he warned that "Pennsylvania and Virginia wish to create a system*

in which they will have enormous and monstrous
influence."

3. The Connecticut Plan

▸ *The divisive issue of representation threatened to dissolve
the convention. "We were on the verge of dissolution,"
wrote Oliver Ellsworth of Connecticut, "scarce held
together by the strength of a hair."*

▸ *Roger Sherman and William Johnson of Connecticut
broke the deadlock by proposing a compromise.
The Connecticut Compromise called for a bicameral
legislature. One body, the House of Representatives
would have representation based on population (the
Virginia Plan), and a second body, the Senate, would
have two members from each state (the New Jersey
Plan).*

4. Consequences

▸ *The Connecticut Compromise successfully resolved the
dispute between the large and small states.*

▸ *The Connecticut Compromise continues to give less
populous states a disproportionate influence in Congress.
The ten most populous states have a total of 20
Senators to represent 53 percent of the U.S. population.
In contrast, the ten least populous states have 20
Senators to represent 3 percent of the U.S. population.*

C. THE THREE-FIFTHS COMPROMISE

1. The Southern Position

▸ *The slave population was concentrated in the South.
Over 90 percent of all slaves lived in Georgia, Maryland,
North Carolina, South Carolina, and Virginia. Slaves
accounted for 30 percent of the total population of these
states.*

▸ *Southern delegates demanded that slaves be counted in
determining representation in Congress.*

2. The Northern Position

▸ *Many Northern delegates opposed slavery. For example,
Gouverneur Morris of Pennsylvania called slavery, "a
nefarious institution. It is the curse of heaven on the
states where it prevails."*

▸ *Other Northern delegates questioned how property could be a rule of representation. Eldridge Gerry of Massachusetts asked, "Why then should the blacks, who are property in the South, be in the rule of presentation more than the cattle and horses of the North?"*

3. The Three-Fifths Compromise
   ▸ *The Framers agreed that all "free persons" and "three-fifths of all other persons" should be counted for representation in Congress.*
   ▸ *The Framers also agreed that the same formula would be used to determine taxation.*
4. Consequences
   ▸ *The Three-Fifths Compromise temporarily defused the tensions between the North and South.*
   ▸ *The Thirteenth Amendment ultimately abolished slavery, thus eliminating the Three-Fifths Compromise.*

D. ECONOMIC POWERS

1. The Framers assigned a high priority to economic issues. They agreed on the need for a strong national government to promote economic growth and protect property.
2. The Framers adopted a number of provisions to increase the economic power of the central government. For example, Congress was given the power to:
   ▸ *Obtain revenue through taxing*
   ▸ *Pay debts*
   ▸ *Coin money and regulate its value*
   ▸ *Regulate interstate and foreign commerce*
   ▸ *Establish uniform laws of bankruptcy*
   ▸ *Punish counterfeiting*
   ▸ *Establish post offices*

E. INDIVIDUAL RIGHTS

1. Delegates agreed on the importance of safeguarding individual rights.
2. The Constitution includes the following protections of individual rights:
   ▸ *It prohibits suspension of habeas corpus. A writ of habeas corpus is a court order requiring that an*

individual in custody be brought into court and shown the cause for detention.

▸ *It prohibits Congress or the states from passing bills of attainder. A bill of attainder is a legislative act that inflicts punishment without a court trial.*

▸ *It prohibits Congress or the states from passing ex post facto laws. An ex post facto law punishes a person for acts that were not illegal when the act was committed.*

▸ *It upholds the right to trial by jury in criminal cases.*

▸ *It prohibits the imposition of religious qualifications for holding office.*

V. THE THREE BRANCHES OF GOVERNMENT

A. SEPARATING POWERS

1. The Framers accepted Montesquieu's position that power must be used to balance power.

2. The Framers believed that separating power into legislative, executive, and judicial branches would provide an indispensable defense against tyranny.

B. THE LEGISLATIVE BRANCH

1. Article I of the Constitution called for a bicameral Congress consisting of two chambers—a House of Representatives and a Senate.

2. Chapter 10 provides a detailed discussion of Congress and the legislative branch.

C. THE EXECUTIVE BRANCH

1. Article II of the Constitution called for an executive branch led by a President chosen by an electoral college.

2. Chapter 11 provides a detailed discussion of the presidency and the executive branch.

D. THE JUDICIAL BRANCH

1. Article III of the Constitution called for a judicial branch with a Supreme Court as the highest court of the national government.
2. Chapter 13 provides a detailed discussion of the Supreme Court and the judicial branch.

VI. CHECKS AND BALANCES

A. PURPOSE

1. The Constitution calls for a national government with legislative, executive, and judicial branches.
2. The three branches, however, are not completely separate. Instead they are tied together by an elaborate system of checks and balances that are designed to implement the Framers' goal of setting power against power to thwart tyranny and restrain irresponsible majorities.

B. EXAMPLES

1. Congress and the President
   - *Congress has the power to make law, but the President may veto or reject an act of Congress.*
   - *Congress can override a presidential veto by a two-thirds vote in each house.*
   - *The President negotiates treaties that must be ratified by the Senate.*
2. Congress, the President, and the Supreme Court
   - *The President has the power to nominate justices to the Supreme Court.*
   - *The Senate has the power to approve or reject presidential nominations.*
   - *The Supreme Court can use its power of judicial review to declare laws and presidential acts unconstitutional.*
   - *The Congress can propose a constitutional amendment to reverse a Supreme Court ruling.*

KEY CONTENT REVIEW

> ▸ *The House of Representatives may, by majority vote, impeach Supreme Court justices and the President. The Senate may, by a two-thirds vote, convict and remove Supreme Court justices and the President.*

C. CONSEQUENCES

1. The system of checks and balances slows change and encourages compromise.
2. The system of checks and balances means that the three branches are not completely independent.

> The Constitution describes a number of specific checks and balances. Test writers often include a multiple-choice question asking students to identify an example of a constitutional check and balance.

VII. LIMITATIONS ON MAJORITY RULE

A. THE PROBLEM OF EXCESSIVE DEMOCRACY

1. Majority rule is one of the hallmarks of a democratic system of government. However, leading Framers such as James Madison and Alexander Hamilton feared that majorities could abuse their power.
2. The unruly mobs in Shays's Rebellion and the radical legislators in Rhode Island provided ample proof of the dangers posed by "excessive democracy."

B. WAYS THE CONSTITUTION LIMITS MAJORITY RULE

1. An insulated Senate
   > ▸ *The Framers viewed the Senate as a bulwark against irresponsible majorities in the House of Representatives.*
   > ▸ *State legislatures originally chose senators. (This practice was later changed when the Seventeenth Amendment*

established the direct election of senators by popular majorities.)

▸ *The staggered term of service in the Senate made it more resistant to popular pressures.*

▸ *The Framers believed that the Senate would check popular passions expressed in the House of Representatives. Washington later explained this function to Jefferson when he asked, "Why did you pour that coffee into your saucer?" "To cool it," Jefferson replied. "Even so," said Washington, "we pour legislation into the senatorial saucer to cool it."*

2. An independent judiciary

▸ *The judicial branch is insulated from popular control.*

▸ *Federal judges are appointed by the President and confirmed by the Senate.*

▸ *Federal judges serve until they resign, retire, or die in office. They can be removed from office only through the impeachment process.*

3. An indirectly elected President

▸ *The President is not directly elected by the popular vote.*

▸ *Instead, the Framers created an electoral college comprised of electors who would then choose a "distinguished character of continental reputation." (The electors are now "rubber stamps" who follow the popular majority in their states.)*

VIII. THE FIGHT FOR RATIFICATION

A. THE PROCESS

1. The Articles of Confederation could be amended only by the agreement of all 13 state legislatures.
2. In contrast, the Framers required that conventions in only 9 of the 13 states would be needed to approve the Constitution.
3. Ratification sparked a nationwide debate between Anti-Federalists who opposed the Constitution and Federalists who supported it.

B. THE ANTI-FEDERALISTS

1. Included small farmers, shopkeepers, and laborers
2. Favored strong state governments and weak national governments.
3. Called for a Bill of Rights to protect individual liberties.

C. THE FEDERALISTS

1. Included large landowners, wealthy merchants, and professionals.
2. Favored weaker state governments and a strong national government.
3. Promised to add amendments specifically protecting individual liberties.

D. THE *FEDERALIST PAPERS*

1. A series of 85 essays written by Alexander Hamilton, James Madison, and John Jay to support the Constitution.
2. In the *Federalist No. 10*, James Madison argued that political factions are undesirable but inevitable. Madison believed that the excesses of factionalism could be limited by the system of republican representation created by the Constitution.
3. Madison also argued that a large republic such as the United States would fragment political power and thus curb the threat posed by the non-wealthy majority.

Political scientists now agree that the Federalist Papers *influenced few of the New York delegates to ratify the Constitution. However, the* Federalist Papers *have had a significant influence on the AP U.S. Government and Politics Development Committee. Most exams include a multiple-choice question devoted to Madison's contention that political factions are undesirable but inevitable. Reading* Federalist No. 10 *and* No. 51 *will help you prepare for free-response questions on the theoretical underpinnings of the Constitution.*

E. RATIFICATION

1. Although Delaware, New Jersey, and other small states promptly ratified the Constitution, the contest proved to be very close in Virginia and New York.
2. North Carolina and Rhode Island insisted on a bill of rights as a condition for joining the Union.
3. The First Congress ratified ten amendments collectively known as the Bill of Rights. See Chapters 15, 16, and 17 for a detailed discussion of the Bill of Rights.

IX. CONSTITUTIONAL CHANGE

A. THE FORMAL AMENDMENT PROCESS

1. Methods of proposal
   - *By two-thirds vote in both houses of Congress.*
   - *By a national constitutional convention called by Congress at the request of two-thirds of the state legislatures. (This method has never been used.)*
2. Methods of ratification
   - *By legislatures in three-fourths of the states.*
   - *By conventions in three-fourths of the states.*
3. Key points
   - *The procedures for formally amending the Constitution illustrate the federal structure of American government. See Chapter 4 for a full discussion of federalism.*
   - *The procedure for formally amending the Constitution requires the support of supermajorities in both Congress and the states.*

B. INFORMAL METHODS OF CONSTITUTIONAL CHANGE

1. Congressional legislation
   - *Congress has passed a number of laws that both clarify and expand constitutional provisions.*
   - *The Judiciary Act of 1789 began the process of creating the federal court system we have today. See Chapter 13 for a detailed discussion of the federal court system.*

> ▸ *Acts of Congress created the cabinet departments, agencies, and offices in the executive branch. See Chapters 11 and 12 for a detailed discussion of the executive branch.*
>
> ▸ *Congress has passed a number of laws that have defined and expanded the Commerce Clause. For example, congressional regulations now cover railroad lines, air routes, and Internet traffic. In addition, Congress used the Commerce Clause to ban discrimination in public accommodations. See Chapter 16 for a detailed discussion of the Civil Rights Act of 1964.*

2. Executive actions

> ▸ *Presidents have used their power as commander-in-chief of the armed forces to send troops into combat without a declaration of war.*
>
> ▸ *An executive agreement is a pact made by the President with the head of a foreign state. Unlike treaties, executive agreements do not have to be ratified by the Senate. Presidents often use executive agreements to circumvent the formal treaty-making process described in the Constitution.*

3. Judicial decisions

> ▸ *Judicial review is the power of the Supreme Court to determine if acts of Congress and the President are in accord with the Constitution.*
>
> ▸ *Judicial review is not specifically described in the Constitution.*
>
> ▸ *The Supreme Court claimed the power of judicial review in* Madison v. Marbury *in 1803. See Chapter 13 for a detailed discussion of judicial review.*

4. Party practices

> ▸ *Political parties are not mentioned in the Constitution. In fact, the Framers warned of what George Washington called "the baneful effects of the spirit of party."*
>
> ▸ *Since the 1830s, political parties have held conventions to nominate candidates for President. As a result, the electoral college had become a "rubber stamp" for the popular vote in each state. See Chapter 7 for a detailed discussion of political parties.*

▸ *Political parties now determine how congressional committees are organized and led. See Chapter 10 for a detailed discussion of the role that political parties play in Congress.*

5. Unwritten traditions

▸ *According to the Constitution, the President has the power to nominate federal judges who are approved by the Senate.*

▸ *The unwritten tradition of senatorial courtesy requires the President to first seek the approval of the senator or senators of the President's party from the state in which the nominee will serve.*

Federalism

 I. **THREE SYSTEMS OF GOVERNMENT**

A. UNITARY

1. A centralized system of government in which all power is vested in a central government.
2. Most nations in the world today have unitary governments. For example, Great Britain, France, and China all have unitary governments.

B. CONFEDERATE

1. A decentralized system of government in which a weak central government has limited power over the states.
2. The United States began as a confederation under the Articles of Confederation. The United Nations is a modern example of a confederation.

C. FEDERAL

1. A system of government in which power is divided by a written constitution between a central government and regional governments. As a result, two or more levels of government have formal authority over the same area and people.
2. The United States, Mexico, Canada, Germany and India all have federal systems of government.

II. THE CONSTITUTIONAL DIVISION OF POWERS

A. THE FRAMERS CHOOSE FEDERALISM

1. The Framers agreed that the confederate system of government under the Articles of Confederation proved to be too weak to deal with the new nation's myriad problems.

2. The Framers ruled out a unitary system of government because the Revolution had been fought against a distant central government in London.

3. The Framers chose to balance order and freedom by creating a federal system that assigned powers to the national government while reserving other powers to the states.

B. EXPRESSED POWERS

1. Expressed powers (also called enumerated powers) are specifically granted to the federal government by the Constitution.

2. Article I, Section 8 lists 18 separate clauses that enumerate 27 powers to Congress. Article II, Section 2 assigns the President several expressed powers. Article III grants "the judicial power of the United States" to the Supreme Court. And finally, several amendments contain expressed powers. For example, the Sixteenth Amendment gives Congress the power to levy an income tax.

3. Key expressed powers
   ▸ *The power to regulate interstate and foreign commerce.*
   ▸ *The power to tax and spend.*
   ▸ *The war power.*

C. IMPLIED POWERS

1. Implied powers are not expressly stated in the Constitution.

2. Implied powers are derived from Article I, Section 8, Clause 18. Known as the elastic clause or necessary and proper clause, this key provision gives Congress the power "to make all Laws which shall be necessary and proper for carrying into Execution the forgoing Powers and all other Powers vested by the Constitution in the Government of the United States, or in any Department or Officer thereof."

3. The necessary and proper clause enables the national government to meet problems the Framers could not anticipate. It thus insured the growth of national power by enabling the federal government to extend its powers beyond those enumerated in the Constitution.

D. INHERENT POWERS

1. Inherent powers derive from the fact that the United States is a sovereign nation.
2. Under international law, all nation-states have the right to make treaties, wage war, and acquire territory.

E. RESERVED POWERS

1. Reserved powers are held solely by the states.
2. The Tenth Amendment states, "The powers not delegated to the United States by the Constitution, nor prohibited by it to the states, are reserved to the states respectively, or to the people."
3. Reserve powers include licensing doctors, establishing public schools, and establishing local governments. Reserve powers also include the police power—the authority of a state to protect and promote the public morals, health, safety, and general welfare.

F. CONCURRENT POWERS

1. Concurrent powers are exercised by both national and state governments.
2. Concurrent powers include the power to tax, borrow money, and establish courts.

G. PROHIBITED POWERS

1. Prohibited powers are denied to the national government, state governments, or both.
2. For example, the federal government cannot tax exports, and states cannot make treaties with foreign countries.

MILESTONES IN ESTABLISHING NATIONAL SUPREMACY

A. "THE CARDINAL QUESTION"

1. Woodrow Wilson believed that the relationship between the national government and the states "is the cardinal question of our constitutional system."

2. Wilson further observed that the relationship "cannot be settled by one generation because it is a question of growth, and every successive stage of our political and economic development gives it a new aspect, makes it a new question."

B. *MCCULLOCH V. MARYLAND* (1819) AND IMPLIED POWERS

1. Background of the case
   ▸ *Congress chartered the Second National Bank of the United States in 1816.*
   ▸ *In 1818, the Maryland legislature passed a law imposing a substantial tax on the operation of the Baltimore branch of the bank.*
   ▸ *James McCulloch, cashier of the Baltimore branch, refused to pay the tax.*
   ▸ *When the Maryland state courts ruled against him, McCulloch appealed to the United States Supreme Court.*

2. Constitutional questions
   ▸ *Does the Constitution permit Congress to charter a bank?*
   ▸ *Does a state have a constitutional right to tax an agency of the United States government?*

3. The Court's decision
   ▸ *Led by Chief Justice John Marshall, the Supreme Court ruled that creating a national bank was within the implied powers of Congress. Marshall acknowledged that the word* bank *is not in the Constitution. However, the Constitution does specifically grant Congress the power to impose taxes, issue a currency, and borrow money. Although the Constitution does not specifically enumerate creating a bank, it does grant Congress the power to "make all laws necessary and proper for carrying into execution the foregoing powers." Congress*

may thus reasonably decide that chartering a national bank is a "necessary and proper" way to carry out its expressed powers.

▸ *The Court also held that the Maryland law was unconstitutional because it violated the principle of the supremacy of the national government over the states. Marshall ruled that "the government of the United States, though limited in its power, is supreme within its sphere of action."*

4. Significance

▸ McCulloch v. Maryland *confirmed the right of Congress to utilize implied powers to carry out its expressed powers. Federal programs to build interstate highways, regulate labor-management relations, and inspect food and drugs are all justified as implied powers of Congress.*

▸ *The decision validated the supremacy of the national government over the states by declaring that states cannot interfere with or tax the legitimate activities of the federal government.*

C. NULLIFICATION AND THE CIVIL WAR

1. John C. Calhoun of South Carolina argued that a state can nullify or refuse to recognize an act of Congress that it considered unconstitutional.

2. The Civil War was both a conflict over slavery and a dispute over the relationship between the Southern states and the national government.

3. The Civil War forcibly refuted the doctrine of nullification while also confirming that the federal union is indissoluble.

D. *GIBBONS V. OGDEN* (1824) AND THE COMMERCE CLAUSE

1. Background of the case

▸ *The New York legislature granted Aaron Ogden an "exclusive license" to run a ferry service on the Hudson River between New York and New Jersey.*

▸ *Thomas Gibbons obtained a license from the federal government to operate a competing New York–New Jersey ferry service.*

> ‣ *Ogden claimed that Gibbons infringed on the monopoly rights granted to him by the New York legislature.*
> ‣ *When the New York courts ruled against him, Gibbons appealed to the United States Supreme Court.*

2. Constitutional questions
> ‣ *Did the New York law violate the Constitution by attempting to regulate interstate commerce?*
> ‣ *Does Congress have the exclusive right to regulate interstate commerce?*

3. The Court's decision
> ‣ *Led by Chief Justice John Marshall, the Supreme Court defined commerce as all commercial business dealings. Commerce thus includes the production, buying, selling, renting, and transporting of goods, services, and properties.*
> ‣ *Because Congress regulates all interstate commerce, the Court upheld Gibbons' right to operate a ferry service in competition with Ogden.*

4. Significance
> ‣ *Marshall's broad definition of commerce enabled Congress to promote economic growth by supporting the construction of roads, canals, and railroad lines.*

E. THE EXPANSION OF THE COMMERCE CLAUSE

1. The commerce clause has played a key role in the expansion of federal power.
2. The national government now regulates a wide variety of commercial activities, including radio signals, telephone messages, and financial transactions.
3. The Supreme Court upheld the 1964 Civil Rights Act forbidding discrimination in places of public accommodation such as restaurants and hotels on the basis of its power to regulate interstate commerce.

Test Tip

The commerce clause and the elastic clause have played key roles in the expansion of federal power. Be sure you can give examples of how these clauses have been used to increase the power of the federal government relative to the power of state governments. For example, the Supreme Court used the commerce clause to uphold the 1964 Civil Rights Act.

F. THE STRUGGLE OVER SCHOOL DESEGREGATION

1. In 1954, in *Brown v. Board of Education*, the Supreme Court unanimously held that school segregation was unconstitutional.
2. President Eisenhower sent federal troops to Little Rock's Central High School to enforce court-ordered desegregation.
3. Despite initial resistance, national standards of racial equality ultimately prevailed.

IV. INTERGOVERNMENTAL RELATIONS

A. DUAL FEDERALISM

1. A system of government in which the national and state governments remain supreme within their own spheres. For example, the national government is responsible for foreign policy, while the states have exclusive responsibility for the public schools.
2. Dual federalism is often called "layer cake" federalism. It characterized the relationship between the nation and the state governments until the advent of the New Deal during the 1930s.

B. COOPERATIVE FEDERALISM

1. A system of government in which the national and state governments work together to complete projects. For example, the interstate highway program features a partnership in which national and state governments share costs and administrative duties.
2. Cooperative federalism is often called "marble cake" federalism because of the blurred distinction between the levels of government.

C. FISCAL FEDERALISM

1. Refers to the pattern of spending, taxing, and providing grants in the federal system.

2. In 2010, state and local governments received about $480 billion in federal grants. These grants accounted for about 21 percent of all funds spent by state and local governments.

3. Types of federal grants

   ▸ *Categorical grants—made for specific, carefully defined purposes. Examples include money spent to build interstate highways and wastewater treatment plants.*

   ▸ *Block grants—made for a broadly defined purpose. Block grants give the states broad discretion in how the money will be spent. Examples include money given to the states for homeland security and community development.*

Test Tip

It is very important to understand the differences between categorical and block grants. Categorical grants are designed for a specific purpose. They have increased the power of the federal government because states must comply with the attendant regulations. In contrast, block grants have fewer strings attached, thus allowing states greater discretion in making decisions about how to implement a program.

4. Mandates

   ▸ *A mandate is a rule telling states what they must do to comply with federal guidelines.*

   ▸ *Civil rights and environmental protection are the most common mandates. For example, state programs may not discriminate against people because of their race, sex, age, or ethnicity.*

   ▸ *An unfunded mandate requires state and local governments to provide services without providing resources for these services. For example, the 1986 Handicapped Children's Protection Act required public schools to build access ramps and provide special buses, but the act did not provide federal funds to pay for these additions.*

D. DEVOLUTION

1. Refers to a movement to transfer responsibilities of governing from the federal government to state and local governments.
2. For example, the Welfare Reform Act of 1996 gave the states the money to run their own welfare programs. States had wide discretion in implementing the federal goal of transferring people from welfare to work.

V. ADVANTAGES AND DISADVANTAGES OF FEDERALISM

A. ADVANTAGES

1. Promotes diverse policies that encourage experimentation and creative ideas.
2. Provides multiple power centers, thus making it difficult for any one faction or interest group to dominate government policies.
3. Keeps the government close to the people by increasing opportunities for political participation.

B. DISADVANTAGES

1. Promotes inequality because states differ in the resources they can devote to providing services.
2. Enables local interests to delay or even thwart majority support for a policy.
3. Creates confusion because the different levels of government make it difficult for citizens to know what different governments are doing.

Political Beliefs and Public Opinion

 I. **AMERICAN POLITICAL CULTURE**

A. KEY DEFINITIONS

1. Political culture—a set of widely shared political beliefs and values.
2. Values and beliefs—deep-rooted ideals that shape an individual's perception of political issues.
3. Opinion—a specific view about a particular issue or event.
4. Public opinion—attitudes about institutions, leaders, political issues, and events.

B. IMPORTANCE

1. The British political writer G. K. Chesterton observed that "America is the only nation in the world that is founded on a creed."
2. America's political culture provides a broad consensus that shapes and limits the public debate about political issues.

C. CORE VALUES

1. Liberty/Freedom
    ▸ *Freedom of speech and religion are fundamental parts of the American political culture.*
    ▸ *People should be free to lead their lives with minimal government interference.*
2. Equality
    ▸ *Political equality—all adult citizens should have equal voting rights.*

> ▶ *Legal equality—everyone is entitled to equal treatment before the law.*
> ▶ *Equality of opportunity—all Americans should have a chance to succeed in life.*

   3. Individualism

> ▶ *Respect for the dignity and importance of each individual.*
> ▶ *People should be responsible for their own decisions and well-being.*

   4. Democracy

> ▶ *Government should be based on the consent of the governed.*
> ▶ *The majority has a right to rule.*
> ▶ *The rights of the minority should be respected and protected.*
> ▶ *Citizens have a responsibility to support their local communities.*

> **AP U.S. Government and Politics test writers often write multiple-choice questions asking students to identify an answer that is NOT a core value of American political culture. It is important to remember that, while America's political culture does support economic opportunity, it does NOT support economic equality.**

D. MISTRUST OF GOVERNMENT

1. Since the 1950s, Americans have become less trusting of their leaders and political institutions.
2. The mistrust of government is linked to a corresponding decline in political efficacy, the belief that one's political participation really matters.

II. POLITICAL SOCIALIZATION

A. IMPORTANCE

1. Political socialization is a continuing process that is vital to societies and to individuals.

2. It is the process by which political values are formed and passed from one generation to the next.

B. AGENTS OF SOCIALIZATION

1. The family
   - ▸ *The family is the most important agent of political socialization.*
   - ▸ *Children raised in households in which both parents strongly identify with the same political party are likely to identify with their parents' party.*

2. Education
   - ▸ *Class elections, student government, and social studies classes play a key role in teaching students the values of liberty, equality, individualism, and democracy.*
   - ▸ *College graduates have a higher level of political participation than do other Americans.*

3. Social groups
   - ▸ *Black and white Americans differ on a number of issues, including affirmative action programs and race relations.*
   - ▸ *Religious groups differ on a number of issues, including same-sex marriage, school prayer, and abortion.*
   - ▸ *Men and women differ on a number of issues, including health care programs and support for defense budgets.*

Test Tip

Most of the released exams have included a multiple-choice question asking students to either define political socialization or recognize that the family plays the most important role in passing political values from one generation to the next.

III. POLITICAL IDEOLOGY

A. IMPORTANCE

1. A political ideology is a cohesive set of beliefs about politics, public policy, and the role of government.

KEY CONTENT REVIEW

2. Although political ideology is important to politicians and activists, studies consistently find that only about 20 percent of Americans vote along ideological lines.

B. LIBERAL IDEOLOGY

1. Supports
   ▸ *Political and social reform*
   ▸ *Government regulation of the economy*
   ▸ *Expanded programs for the poor, minorities, and women*
   ▸ *National health care system*
   ▸ *Abortion rights*
2. Opposes
   ▸ *Increases in military spending*
   ▸ *Committing troops to foreign wars*
   ▸ *School prayer*

C. CONSERVATIVE IDEOLOGY

1. Supports
   ▸ *Expansion of American military power*
   ▸ *Free-market solutions to economic problems*
   ▸ *Less government regulation of business*
   ▸ *School prayer*
2. Opposes
   ▸ *Expensive federal social and welfare programs*
   ▸ *Abortion rights*
   ▸ *National health care system*

IV. THE SCIENCE OF PUBLIC OPINION MEASUREMENT

A. A BRIEF HISTORY OF POLLING

1. Straw polling
   ▸ *American political leaders have a long history of trying to gauge public opinion.*
   ▸ *Early attempts included counting the size of a crowd, noting the level of audience applause, and asking random people on the street to express their opinion.*

▸ *These tactics are all called straw polling. The name comes from the practice of tossing straw into the air to see which way the wind is blowing.*

2. The *Literary Digest* fiasco

   ▸ *In 1936, a widely read periodical, the* Literary Digest, *mailed postcard ballots to more than 10 million people asking if they supported Franklin D. Roosevelt or his Republican challenger, Alf Landon.*

   ▸ *The overwhelming majority of the 2 million survey respondents supported Landon. Based on this response, the* Literary Digest *confidently predicted that Landon would win a landslide victory. Much to the magazine's shock and embarrassment, Roosevelt won an overwhelming victory, carrying every state but Maine and Vermont.*

   ▸ *The* Literary Digest *poll produced flawed results because it relied on a faulty sample that used telephone directories and automobile registration rosters. The* Literary Digest *pollsters failed to consider that, during the Great Depression, millions of working-class Americans could not afford telephones or automobiles. The poll thus excluded Roosevelt's blue-collar supporters while oversampling wealthy Americans who supported Landon.*

3. Scientific sampling

   ▸ *George Gallup and Elmo Roper developed the technique of scientific sampling.*

   ▸ *Today, over 1,000 polling organizations attempt to measure public preferences on everything from soft drinks to soap operas. Led by the Gallup Organization and the Pew Research Center for People and the Press, as many as 200 organizations focus on polling the American public's political preferences.*

B. STEPS IN SCIENTIFIC POLLING

1. Define the universe or population to be surveyed.

2. Construct a sample or representative slice of the population. Most polls use random sampling in which every member of the population being studied must have an equal chance of being sampled. If this happens, a small sample should represent the whole population.

3. Construct carefully designed survey questions that avoid bias.

4. Conduct the poll by using either telephone or face-to-face interviewing procedures.

5. Analyze and report the data.

V. POLLS AND DEMOCRACY

A. A TOOL FOR DEMOCRACY

1. Supporters argue that polling contributes to the democratic process by providing a way for the public to express its opinions.

2. Supporters also point out that polling enables political leaders to understand and implement public preferences on key issues.

B. A TOOL FOR THE TIMID AND MANIPULATIVE

1. Critics argue that polls transform leaders into followers. For example, had polls been available in 1787, the Framers might have been content to follow public opinion by revising the Articles of Confederation.

2. Critics also charge that polls can be used to manipulate public opinion. For example, the bandwagon effect occurs when polling results influence people to support candidates and issues that appear to be popular.

C. A CAUTION FOR THE DEMOCRATIC PROCESS

1. The democratic process is based on an informed citizenry.

2. Public opinion polls reveal an alarming lack of public knowledge about the American political system.

   ▸ *A national poll found that 74 percent of respondents could name the Three Stooges, while just 42 percent could identify the three branches of government.*

   ▸ *Another major study found that only 25 percent of respondents could name their two senators and less than half knew that the Constitution's first ten amendments are called the Bill of Rights.*

Voters and Voter Behavior

I. THE EXPANSION OF VOTING RIGHTS

A. TWO LONG-TERM TRENDS

1. Federal laws and constitutional amendments have eliminated restrictions on the right to vote, thus dramatically expanding the American electorate.
2. Federal laws and constitutional amendments have significantly reduced the power of individual states over a citizen's right to vote.

B. THE ORIGINAL ELECTORATE

1. In 1789, property and tax qualifications restricted the electorate to white male property owners.
2. Only about one in fifteen adult white males had the right to vote.

C. JACKSONIAN DEMOCRACY

1. Andrew Jackson and his supporters had great respect for the common sense and abilities of the common man. As a result, the Jacksonians eliminated property ownership and tax payments as qualifications for voting.
2. By 1850, almost all white adult males had the right to vote.

D. THE FIFTEENTH AMENDMENT, 1870

1. The Fifteenth Amendment prohibited voting restrictions based on "race, color, or previous condition of servitude."

2. Despite the Fifteenth Amendment, a combination of literary tests, poll taxes, white primaries, and the grandfather clause systematically disenfranchised African Americans. For a detailed discussion of these measures, see Chapter 16.

E. THE NINETEENTH AMENDMENT, 1920

1. Prior to 1920, women had full voting rights in New York and a number of Western states.
2. The Nineteenth Amendment removed voting restrictions based on gender.

F. THE TWENTY-THIRD AMENDMENT, 1961

1. Prior to 1961, residents of the District of Columbia could not vote in presidential elections.
2. The Twenty-Third Amendment added voters of the District of Columbia to the presidential electorate.

G. THE TWENTY-FOURTH AMENDMENT, 1964

1. Prior to 1964, a number of states used poll taxes as a means of discouraging citizens from voting.
2. The Twenty-Fourth Amendment outlawed the poll tax "or any tax" as a qualification for voting.

H. THE VOTING RIGHTS ACT OF 1965

1. Prohibited any government from using voting procedures that denied a person the vote on the basis of race or color.
2. Abolished the use of literacy requirements for anyone who had completed the sixth grade.
3. Authorized federal registrars to protect African Americans' right to vote in Southern states and counties with histories of discrimination.
4. For a detailed discussion of the Voting Rights Act of 1965, see Chapter 16.

I. THE TWENTY-SIXTH AMENDMENT, 1971

1. The Twenty-Sixth Amendment provides that the minimum age for voting in any election cannot be less than 18 years.

2. Note that a state may set a minimum voting age of less than 18.

II. FACTORS THAT INFLUENCE TURNOUT AND VOTER CHOICES

A. EDUCATION

1. People with more education are more likely to vote. People with less education are less likely to vote.
2. Historically, as the level of voters' education increases, the percentage voting Republican increases. However, the 2008 presidential election proved to be an exception to this trend because slightly more college graduates voted for the Democratic candidate Barack Obama than the Republican candidate John McCain.

B. INCOME

1. People with more income are more likely to vote. In contrast, people with less income are less likely to vote.
2. Historically, voters in lower income brackets are more likely to support Democrats, while voters in higher income brackets are more likely to support Republicans. In the 2008 presidential election, however, voters with annual incomes of $50,000 or more were evenly split between Barack Obama and John McCain.

C. AGE

1. Older people are more likely to vote than are younger people. Note that voter turnout does decrease over the age of 70 and that turnout among voters age 18 to 24 is beginning to increase.
2. Historically, young voters are more likely to support Democratic candidates, while older voters are more likely to support Republican candidates.

KEY CONTENT REVIEW

|53

D. GENDER

1. Women vote at higher percentages than men. In the 2008 presidential election, women comprised 54 percent of all voters.

2. Women generally favor the Democrats, while men generally favor the Republicans. Known as the gender gap, this phenomenon first appeared in the 1980s.

E. RELIGION

1. Jews and Catholics are more likely to vote than Protestants.

2. Historically, a majority of Protestants have supported Republican candidates, while a majority of Jewish and Catholic voters have supported Democratic candidates.

F. RACE

1. Whites tend to have higher turnout rates than do African Americans, Hispanics, and other minority groups. It is important to note that when the effects of income and education are eliminated, black citizens vote at a higher rate than do white citizens.

2. The presidency of Franklin D. Roosevelt witnessed a major shift of African American voters from the Republican Party to the Democratic Party. The overwhelming majority of African Americans now support Democratic candidates. Note that African American Democrats tend to support the more liberal candidates within their party.

The AP U.S. Government and Politics exam has included several questions about race and voting. Multiple-choice questions focus on the fact that African Americans strongly support Democratic presidential and congressional candidates. Free-response questions focus on the methods that states used to reduce African American turnout prior to the passage of the Voting Rights Act of 1965.

G. CROSS-PRESSURES

1. Voters belong to more than one group.
2. It is important to note that anything that produces cross-pressures reduces voter turnout.

III. NONVOTING

A. KEY STATISTICS

1. At the present time, there are approximately 230 million people of voting age in the United States.
2. Only about 60 percent of eligible voters actually voted in the 2008 presidential election.
3. The majority of the U.S. electorate does not vote in a nonpresidential election.
4. The voter turnout rate in the United States is lower than in most other Western democracies.

B. FACTORS THAT DECREASE VOTER TURNOUT

1. Voter registration
   ‣ *With the exception of North Dakota, all states have voter registration laws requiring eligible voters to first place their name on an electoral roll in order to be allowed to vote.*
   ‣ *Registration laws have significantly reduced fraud. However, they have created an obstacle that discourages some people from voting.*
   ‣ *The National Voter Registration Act of 1993 (also known as the Motor Voter Act) made voter registration easier by allowing people to register to vote while applying for or renewing a driver's license.*
2. A decline in political efficacy
   ‣ *Political efficacy is the belief that political participation and voting can make a difference.*
   ‣ *Citizens who have a low level of political efficacy believe that their votes will have no effect on the outcome of an election.*

> *A rising level of cynicism and a corresponding decline in trust of government have combined to reduce political efficacy and lower voter turnout rates.*

3. Frequent elections
   > *America's federal system produces more elections than any other modern democracy.*
   > *The large number of elections reduces voter turnout by making it difficult for citizens to keep up with all the candidates running for office.*

4. Weekday, nonholiday voting
   > *Many Western democracies hold elections on weekends and on national holidays.*
   > *Most elections in the United States are held on the first Tuesday after the first Monday in November. Holding elections on a weekday makes it difficult for many people to leave work in order to vote.*

Test Tip

Voting in presidential elections is the most common form of political activity undertaken by U.S. citizens. Nonetheless, a majority of the American electorate does not vote in elections at all levels of government. Remember that voter turnout in the United States is lower than in most other Western democracies.

Political Parties

 I. **INTRODUCTION**

A. WHAT IS A POLITICAL PARTY?

A political party is a group of citizens who organize to:

1. Win elections
2. Hold public offices
3. Operate the government
4. Determine public policy

B. LEVELS OF AMERICAN POLITICAL PARTIES

1. The party in the electorate includes citizens who identify themselves as Democrats or Republicans.
2. The party organization includes national leaders, state chairpersons, county chairpersons, and other activists who run the party at the national, state, and local levels. It is important to remember that the national, state, and local party organizations are independent and not centrally controlled.
3. The party in government includes the party's candidates and office holders.

C. FUNCTIONS OF PARTIES

1. Recruiting and nominating candidates for public office
2. Running political campaigns
3. Articulating positions on issues
4. Critiquing the policies of the party in power

5. Serving as a linking institution that connects citizens to government by:
    ‣ *Providing information to voters about candidates running for office*
    ‣ *Mobilizing voters to elect party candidates*
    ‣ *Raising funds to support party candidates*

D. TYPES OF PARTY SYSTEMS

1. One-party systems
    ‣ *A political system in which one party exercises total control over the government.*
    ‣ *China, North Korea, and Iran all have one-party systems.*
2. Multiparty systems
    ‣ *A political system in which a number of political parties compete for political offices.*
    ‣ *Parties in a multiparty system often represent widely different ideologies about government policies.*
    ‣ *France, Italy, and Israel all have multiparty systems.*
3. Two-party systems
    ‣ *A political system in which two major political parties compete for control of public offices.*
    ‣ *The United States is one of about 15 nations with two-party systems. Other nations include the United Kingdom, India, and Jamaica.*

II. REASONS WHY AMERICA HAS A TWO-PARTY SYSTEM

A. STRONG CONSENSUS ON CORE POLITICAL VALUES

1. Americans share a strong commitment to a group of core political values that include belief in freedom, political equality, individualism, and equality under the law.
2. America has never had a strong socialist party dedicated to creating an entirely new political system.
3. Most Americans identify themselves as moderates who hold beliefs that fall between liberal and conservative views.

B. SINGLE-MEMBER DISTRICTS

1. Almost all American elections are held in single-member districts in which only one candidate is elected to each office on the ballot.

2. In single-member district elections, the candidate who receives the most votes is the winner. It is important to note the difference between a plurality and a majority. In a plurality election, the winning candidate is the person who receives the most votes. In a majority election, the winning candidate is the person who receives more than half of all votes cast.

3. The winner-take-all, single-member district plurality system is very different than a system based on proportional representation. In a system based on proportional representation, each party is awarded legislative seats in proportion to the vote it receives. For example, in a state with 10 congressional seats, a party receiving 20 percent of the vote would be awarded 2 seats. In contrast, in a winner-take-all, single-member district system, the same party would receive no seats.

4. An electoral system based on winner-take-all, single-member districts discourages the emergence of minor parties by forcing them to wager expensive campaigns with a minimal chance of winning political offices.

5. The electoral system based on single-member districts produces legislatures dominated by two political parties.

The AP U.S. Government and Politics exam committee has written several multiple-choice questions designed to test your knowledge of America's system of winner-take-all, single-member districts. Be sure you know that this system makes it difficult for new parties to emerge, thus preserving the two-party system.

KEY CONTENT REVIEW

C. LEGAL BARRIERS TO THIRD PARTIES

1. The names of Democratic and Republican candidates are automatically placed on state ballots.

2. In contrast, minor party candidates must persuade registered voters to sign petitions in order to have their names placed on the ballot.

D. THE FORCE OF HISTORIC TRADITION

1. America has had a two-party system since 1800.

2. The two-party system has generated self-perpetuating laws and traditions. As a result, it is very difficult for a minor party to become a major force in American politics.

III. PARTY ERAS IN AMERICAN HISTORY

A. KEY TERMS

1. Party era
   ▸ *Historical periods dominated by one party.*
2. Critical election
   ▸ *A national crisis forces voters to confront divisive issues that fracture party coalitions.*
   ▸ *Significant groups of voters change their traditional patterns of party loyalty.*
3. Party realignment
   ▸ *Triggered by a critical election.*
   ▸ *The majority party is displaced by the minority party, thus ushering in a new party era.*

B. THE FIRST PARTY SYSTEM, 1796–1824

1. Led by Alexander Hamilton, the Federalists supported a strong federal government and a national bank. The Federalist coalition included financial, commercial, and manufacturing interests.

2. Led by Thomas Jefferson and James Madison, the Democratic-Republicans supported a limited federal government and opposed the national bank. The Democratic-Republican

coalition included farmers, shopkeepers, laborers, and planters.

3. Jefferson defeated the Federalist president John Adams in 1800. This election marked the first time that a party in power peacefully gave up power after losing an election.

C. JACKSON AND THE DEMOCRATS, 1828–1856

1. Led by Andrew Jackson, the Democratic Party supported voting rights for all white males, opposed the national bank, and used the spoils system to reward party loyalists. The Democratic coalition included debtors, frontier pioneers, and small farmers in the West and South.

2. Led by Henry Clay and Daniel Webster, the Whigs supported high tariffs and the national bank. The Whig coalition included a loose alliance of eastern bankers, merchants, industrialists, and owners of large plantations. The Whigs elected only two presidents: William Henry Harrison in 1840 and Zachary Taylor in 1848.

D. THE REPUBLICAN ERA, 1860–1928

1. The issue of slavery dominated American politics during the 1850s. It split the Democrats and led to the demise of the Whigs.

2. Led by Abraham Lincoln, the Republican Party emerged as the most dynamic antislavery party. In the critical election of 1860, the Republicans elected Lincoln, thus becoming the only party in American history to make the transition from minor party to major party status.

3. The Democrats survived the Civil War by becoming the dominant party in the South. The so-called Solid South remained a fixture of American politics for the next 100 years.

4. The election of 1896 marked a second critical election that transformed American politics. Led by William Jennings Bryan, a Democratic coalition of small Western farmers and emerging labor unions advocated free silver and regulations to control the railroads. Led by William McKinley, a Republican coalition of industrialists, financial monopolies, and small businesspeople backed the gold standard, high tariffs, and industrialization.

KEY CONTENT REVIEW

61

5. McKinley's victory enabled the Republicans to remain America's majority party until the Great Depression.

E. FDR AND THE NEW DEAL COALITION, 1932–1964

1. The Great Depression marked an abrupt end to the era of Republican dominance. Led by Franklin D. Roosevelt, the revived Democrats advocated a program of relief, recovery, and reform known as the New Deal.

2. The New Deal coalition included the following groups:
   ▸ *Urban dwellers*
   ▸ *Labor unions*
   ▸ *Catholics and Jews*
   ▸ *Southerners*
   ▸ *African Americans*
   ▸ *It is important to note that urban dwellers and African Americans had been important parts of the Republican coalition. Their movement into the Democratic Party marked a major party realignment that continues to the present day.*

3. The New Deal coalition did not include Northern business leaders and wealthy industrialists.

F. DIVIDED GOVERNMENT, 1968 TO THE PRESENT

1. The election of Richard Nixon in 1968 marked the beginning of a period of Republican dominance in presidential politics. With the exception of the Carter presidency from 1977 to 1981, the Republicans held the White House from 1969 through 1993.

2. Beginning with the election of Richard Nixon in 1968, the Republicans adopted a "Southern strategy" designed to break the Democratic Party's long dominance in the South. Party realignment gradually occurred as Southern conservatives transferred their loyalty to the Republican Party. By the 2008 election, Republicans held the majority of Southern House and Senate seats.

3. Nixon's election also marked the beginning of a new pattern of divided government. For the first time in the twentieth century, a newly elected president moved into the White

House while the opposition party controlled both houses of Congress.

4. The pattern of divided government has dominated American politics since Nixon's election. From 1969 to 2010, the same party has controlled the presidency and both houses of Congress for just 12 years.

5. The pattern of divided government has had a number of important consequences:
    ▸ *It has heightened partisanship and made it more difficult for moderates to negotiate compromises.*
    ▸ *It has slowed both the confirmation and the legislative processes, thus creating gridlock.*
    ▸ *It has increased public frustration, thus contributing to the decline in trust and confidence in government.*

6. The last half century has witnessed a decline in the percentage of voters who identify themselves as Democrats or Republicans and a rise in the number of voters who identify themselves as independents. As a result, there has been a significant increase in the number of "split-ticket" voters who support candidates of different parties on the same ballot. This process of disengagement of people from political parties is called "party dealignment."

Devote special attention to the era of divided government from 1969 to the present. The causes and consequences of divided government have been tested in several free-response questions.

IV. MINOR PARTIES

A. TYPES OF MINOR PARTIES

1. Parties dominated by charismatic leaders:
    ▸ *Theodore Roosevelt's "Bull Moose" Party or Progressive Party split the Republicans, thus enabling the Democrats to capture the White House.*

> ▸ *George Wallace's American Independent Party expressed the Southern backlash to civil rights demonstrations, urban riots, and antiwar protests.*
> ▸ *Ross Perot's presidential campaigns in 1992 and 1996 expressed widespread public outrage at "politics as usual."*

2. Parties organized around a single issue:
   > ▸ *The Free Soil Party opposed the spread of slavery.*
   > ▸ *The Know Nothings opposed Irish-Catholic immigration.*
   > ▸ *The Right to Life Party opposes abortion.*

3. Parties organized around an ideology:
   > ▸ *The Socialist Party supported labor unions and advocated new laws to regulate big businesses.*
   > ▸ *The Libertarian Party emphasizes individualism and a reduction of government programs.*

B. OBSTACLES TO MINOR PARTY CANDIDATES

1. The winner-take-all format of the electoral college makes it very difficult for a minor party candidate to win the presidency. For example, in 1992 Ross Perot won 19 percent of the vote but did not capture a single electoral vote.

2. Single-member districts make it difficult for minor party candidates to win seats in Congress.

3. Minor party candidates are excluded from presidential debates.

C. THE IMPORTANCE AND IMPACT OF MINOR PARTIES

1. Minor parties express strong views on controversial issues.

2. Minor parties often push major parties to adopt their ideas.

3. Minor parties can play a "spoiler role" by affecting the outcome of a presidential election. For example, many analysts believe that Ralph Nader's Green Party pulled critical support from Al Gore and the Democratic Party in the 2000 presidential election.

Interest Groups

I. INTRODUCTION

A. DEFINITION

1. An interest group is an organization of people whose members share policy views on specific issues and attempt to influence public policy to their benefit.
2. Interest groups operate at every level of government in America's federal system.

B. WAYS INTEREST GROUPS LINK CITIZENS TO GOVERNMENT

1. Interest groups express their members' preferences to government policymakers.
2. Interest groups convey government policy information to their members.
3. Interest groups raise and spend money to influence policymakers.

C. DIFFERENCES BETWEEN INTEREST GROUPS AND POLITICAL PARTIES

1. Political parties nominate candidates, contest elections, and seek to gain control over government. In contrast, interest groups seek to support public officials and influence public policies.
2. Political parties have positions on a wide range of public issues. In contrast, interest groups focus only on specific issues that directly affect their members. As a result, interest groups are able to articulate specific policy positions.

3. Political parties are public organizations that are accountable to the voters. In contrast, interest groups are private organizations that are accountable to their members.

 ## II. TYPES OF INTEREST GROUPS

A. THE EXPLOSION OF INTEREST GROUPS

1. Officials in the legislative and executive branches control the distribution of billions of federal dollars. As a result, most industries, corporations, professions, and unions now have interest groups to represent them in Washington, D.C.
2. The number of interest groups has increased from 6,000 in 1959 to approximately 22,000 in 2010.

B. BUSINESS GROUPS

1. Most large corporations employ lobbyists to monitor legislative activity that may affect their business.
2. The National Association of Manufacturers (NAM) represents 12,000 small and large manufacturers in every industrial sector and in all 50 states. It focuses on legislation affecting labor laws, minimum wages, corporate taxes, and trade regulations.
3. The Chamber of Commerce is the world's largest business federation. It spends $20 million a year lobbying for its 3,000 local chambers and 3 million members.
4. The Business Roundtable is an association of about 150 chief executive officers of leading U.S. corporations with $5 trillion in annual revenues and nearly 10 million employees.

C. LABOR GROUPS

1. The American labor movement reached its peak in 1956 when 33 percent of the nonagricultural work force belonged to a union. Today, 16 million Americans, or about 13 percent of the nonagricultural work force, belong to a union.
2. The American Federation of Labor and Congress of Industrial Organizations (AFL-CIO) is America's largest labor union

both in size and political power. About 10 million workers are members of unions belonging to the AFL-CIO.

D. AGRICULTURAL GROUPS

1. Although farmers comprise less than 2 percent of America's population, their interest groups play an influential role in shaping agricultural policies.
2. The Farm Bureau and the National Farmers Union are broad-based organizations that speak for farmers.
3. Specialized interest groups represent different farm products. For example, the National Milk Producers Federation represents the interests of American dairy farmers.

E. PROFESSIONAL ASSOCIATIONS

1. The National Education Association (NEA) represents 3.2 million public school teachers, support personnel, and retired educators. The NEA is actively involved in the debate over how to implement the No Child Left Behind Act.
2. The American Medical Association (AMA) is the nation's largest association of physicians and medical students. The AMA is actively involved in proposals to reform the health care system.
3. The American Bar Association (ABA) is a voluntary association of 410,000 lawyers and law students. The ABA is actively involved in setting academic standards for law schools and in formulating ethical codes for the legal profession.

F. ENVIRONMENTAL GROUPS

1. Leading environmental interest groups include the Sierra Club, the Audubon Society, and the World Wildlife Fund.
2. Environmental interest groups support wilderness protection, pollution control, and animal rights. They oppose strip mining, nuclear power plants, and offshore drilling.

G. PUBLIC INTEREST GROUPS

1. Over 2,000 groups champion causes that promote the public good. Leading public interest groups include Common Cause and the League of Women Voters.

KEY CONTENT REVIEW

2. Public interest groups support causes such as consumer rights, alternative sources of clean energy, and electoral reform.

H. EQUALITY INTERESTS

1. The National Association for the Advancement of Colored People (NAACP) is one of America's oldest and most influential civil rights organizations. It is dedicated to fighting racial discrimination.

2. The National Organization of Women (NOW) is the largest feminist organization in the United States. Its mission is "to take action to bring women into full participation in society—sharing equal rights, responsibilities and opportunities with men, while living free from discrimination."

I. SINGLE-ISSUE GROUPS

1. Single-issue groups focus their efforts on one issue. For example, the National Right to Life Committee opposes abortion, while Planned Parenthood lobbies for reproductive rights.

2. The National Rifle Association is one of the best known and most influential single-interest groups. It works to uphold the right of people to bear arms for recreation and self-defense. In contrast, the National Coalition to Bar Handguns is a single-interest group dedicated to gun control.

 ## III. INTEREST GROUP GOALS AND STRATEGIES

A. FUNDAMENTAL GOALS

1. Gain access to policymakers.
2. Influence public policy.
3. Support sympathetic policymakers.

B. LOBBYING

1. Definitions
   ▸ *Lobbying is the process by which interest groups attempt to influence the decisions of policymakers.*

▸ *Lobbyists are people who attempt to persuade policymakers to support the goals of an interest group.*

2. Lobbying Congress

▸ *Approximately 30,000 lobbyists currently work in Washington, D.C. They spend over $2 billion a year lobbying Congress.*

▸ *Lobbyists often testify before congressional committees.*

▸ *Lobbyists often provide members of Congress with information on technical issues. One congressional aide described the value of timely information: "My boss demands a speech and a statement for the* Congressional Record *for every bill we introduce or co-sponsor—and we have a lot of bills. I just can't do it all myself. The better lobbyists, when they have a proposal they are pushing, bring it to me along with a couple of speeches, a* Record *insert, and a fact sheet."*

▸ *Lobbyists often meet informally with congressional aides.*

▸ *Lobbyists often bring influential constituents to Washington to discuss important policy matters with their representatives.*

3. Lobbying the executive branch

▸ *Most executive lobbying focuses on presenting a point of view to White House aides and other government officials.*

▸ *Most presidents have created a staff position to provide interest groups with access to their administration.*

▸ *Interest groups direct particular attention to establishing access to regulatory agencies.*

4. Lobbying the courts

▸ *While lobbyists can often meet informally with members of Congress and the executive branch, it would be inappropriate for lobbyists to have an informal meeting with a federal judge who is hearing a case important to the interest group the lobbyists are representing.*

▸ *If interest groups fail to achieve their goals in Congress, they can often take their case to the courts. For example, in the 1950s, Congress repeatedly thwarted the NAACP's efforts to support civil rights legislation. The NAACP responded by sponsoring the* Brown v. Board of Education of Topeka *case. The Supreme Court's landmark decision marked a historic victory for the NAACP, while at the same time encouraging other interest groups to use litigation to achieve their goals.*

▸ *Interest groups are not limited to directly sponsoring a case. They can also file an* amicus curiae *("friend of the court") brief in a case the group is interested in. Amicus briefs consist of written arguments submitted to a court in support of one side of a case.*

▸ *Interest groups now play a prominent role in influencing who is nominated to the federal courts. This is especially true for Supreme Court nominations.*

C. CONTRIBUTING MONEY TO CANDIDATES

1. A political action committee (PAC) is a committee formed by business, labor, or other interest groups to raise money and make contributions to the campaign of political candidates whom they support.

2. The amount of money that PACs can contribute directly to an individual candidate is limited by law. For example, a PAC can contribute a maximum of $5,000 per candidate per election. Elections such as primaries, general elections, and special elections are counted separately.

3. There are currently over 4,600 PACs. Over half of all PACs are sponsored by corporations and business groups.

4. PACs play a particularly significant role in supporting incumbent members of the House of Representatives. PACs typically contribute to the campaigns of House members who serve on committees or subcommittees that consider legislation affecting the interest group.

Test Tip

The AP U.S. Government and Politics Development Committee has included at least one multiple-choice question on PACs on each released exam. It is very important that you understand the function and impact of PACs.

D. SHAPING PUBLIC OPINION

1. Interest groups often undertake expensive public relations campaigns to bring an issue to the public's attention.

2. Interest groups also use advertisements to promote their image as good citizens who protect the environment and care about their communities.

3. Interest groups may also engage in highly visible protest demonstrations designed to draw attention to their cause. While business groups rarely use this grassroots tactic, it has been used effectively by civil rights groups. For example, during the 1960s, civil rights groups used nonviolent marches and sit-ins to direct public attention to the injustices of segregation.

 IV. **FACTORS THAT CONTRIBUTE TO THE SUCCESS OF AN INTEREST GROUP**

A. SIZE

1. Size can be an important asset. A large interest group can marshal its members to email legislators, work in election campaigns, and participate in public protests.

2. Size is not always an asset. Political scientist E.E. Schattschneider noted that "pressure politics is essentially the politics of small groups."

3. Large groups are vulnerable to the free-rider problem. Free riders are people who benefit from an interest group without making any contribution. For example, why should a consumer join a public interest group if he or she will benefit from the group's hard work without joining?

4. As an interest group's size increases, its free-rider problem also increases. Small business groups such as the Business Roundtable are able to organize their members more effectively than a large public interest groups such as Common Cause.

B. INTENSITY

1. Interest groups that contain passionately committed activists tend to be more successful than those groups whose members are less intensely involved.

2. Because of their narrow focus, single-interest groups are able to mobilize members who are intensely committed to the group's goals. For example, both pro-life and pro-choice interest groups have members who are passionately committed to their group's goals.

C. FINANCIAL RESOURCES

1. All interest groups require adequate funding. Money is necessary to hire lobbyists, support PACs, write *amicus curiae* briefs, and pay for a host of other activities.
2. Deep financial resources can compensate for a lack of size and intensity.

V. INTEREST GROUPS AND AMERICAN DEMOCRACY

A. THE POWER ELITE THEORY

1. Power elite theorists believe that a small number of super rich individuals, powerful corporate interest groups, and large financial institutions dominate key policy areas.
2. PACs encourage a close connection between money and politics. Business PACs command immense financial resources that give them both access and influence over policymakers.
3. Power elite theorists point to the recent financial crisis to illustrate their view of the close relationship between Wall Street interests and Washington policymakers. While ordinary Americans received small stimulus checks, Wall Street banks received enormous federal bailouts. As noted by the American Political Science Association, "Citizens with lower or moderate incomes speak with a whisper that is lost on the ears of inattentive government officials, while the advantaged roar with a clarity and consistency that policymakers readily hear and routinely follow."

B. THE PLURALIST THEORY

1. Pluralist theorists argue that many interest groups compete for power in a large number of policy areas. They believe that public policies emerge from bargaining and compromises among competing groups.

2. While elitists point to the concentration of power, pluralists emphasize that America's fragmented federal system and division of power into three branches provides many points of access and influence. As a result, no one group can dominate the entire system.

3. Pluralists point out that interest groups lacking financial resources can use their size and intensity to achieve their goals. For example, a determined interest group that lacks legislative influence can turn to the courts for a favorable decision.

C. THE HYPERPLURALIST THEORY

1. Hyperpluralist theorists argue that there are too many interest groups trying to influence public policy.

2. Hyperpluralists point out that when political leaders try to appease competing interest groups, they often create policies that are confusing and at times contradictory. As a result, legislators avoid making hard choices that are in the national interest. For example, public health groups have successfully convinced the government to launch a vigorous antismoking campaign. At the same time, interest groups representing tobacco farmers have successfully lobbied the government to subsidize their crop.

Be sure that you can compare and contrast elitist, pluralist, and hyperpluralist theories of how the American political system works. All three theories attempt to explain who has power and influence in the United States.

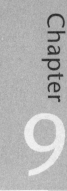

The Mass Media

I. INTRODUCTION

A. KEY DEFINITIONS

1. A medium is a means of communication.
2. *Media* is the plural of *medium*.
3. The mass media are means of communication, such as newspapers, radio, television, and the Internet, that can reach large, widely dispersed audiences.

B. KEY FUNCTIONS OF MASS MEDIA

1. Entertainment
   ‣ *The mass media emphasize entertainment.*
   ‣ *Popular programs are continued, while programs that receive low ratings are cancelled.*
2. News reports
   ‣ *American newspapers have reported political news since the late eighteenth century. For example, newspapers printed the* Federalist Papers *as part of their coverage of the debate over the ratification of the Constitution.*
   ‣ *Radio and television stations provide their audiences with varying degrees of news programming.*
3. Creation of political forums
   ‣ *Politicians use the mass media to promote their careers and draw public attention to their issues.*
   ‣ *The president has direct access to the media and is thus able to use it to help set the policy agenda.*

C. THE MASS MEDIA AS LINKAGE INSTITUTIONS

1. The mass media connect people to their government officials by interviewing citizens, presenting poll results, and covering protests.

2. The mass media connect government officials to the public by interviewing political leaders and reporting on government committees and programs.

> *The mass media, political parties, and interest groups are key linkage institutions. Be sure that you can identify these linkage institutions and explain the ways that they connect citizens to the government.*

II. TYPES OF MASS MEDIA

A. PRINT MEDIA

1. Newspapers
   - ▶ *The* New York Times, Washington Post, *and* Wall Street Journal *are America's most influential newspapers.*
   - ▶ *Most newspapers rely on the Associated Press news agency for national and international stories.*
   - ▶ *Newspaper circulation rates have steadily declined as a result of competition from television and the Internet. In 1960, 50 percent of adults regularly purchased a newspaper. Today, the figure has fallen to just 20 percent.*

2. Magazines
   - ▶ Time, Newsweek, *and* U.S. News & World Report *are America's most widely read and influential news magazines.*
   - ▶ *Magazine circulation rates have fallen sharply as a result of competition from the Internet.*

B. BROADCAST MEDIA

1. Radio

   ▶ *Franklin D. Roosevelt was the first president to take advantage of radio. During the Great Depression, FDR used what he called "fireside chats" to reassure the American people and discuss his New Deal programs.*

   ▶ *Most radio stations now devote little time to reporting political news.*

   ▶ *Within recent years, nationally syndicated talk show hosts have begun to play a prominent and controversial role in discussing political issues. Leading conservative commentators include Rush Limbaugh and Glenn Beck. Leading liberal commentators include Thom Hartmann and Rachel Maddow.*

2. Television

   ▶ *The 1960 presidential debates between Senator John F. Kennedy and Vice President Richard Nixon marked a watershed event when television replaced newspapers and radio as America's principal source of political news.*

   ▶ *Over 98 percent of American households own at least one television.*

   ▶ *The three major networks—NBC, CBS, and ABC—have historically dominated political coverage with their nightly news programs and news specials. However, the networks are experiencing a steady decline of viewership as more and more people turn to cable stations and the Internet.*

   ▶ *Cable networks such as CNN, Fox News, and MSNBC now provide continuous coverage of national and international news.*

3. The Internet

   ▶ *Although television continues to be the most widely used source for political news, the Internet is rapidly becoming a key source of information for the American people.*

   ▶ *The Internet is especially popular among people under the age of 30.*

   ▶ *Many websites such as Politico.com and the Huffington Post provide extensive coverage of political issues and policymakers.*

> ‣ *Web blogs now facilitate rapid communication between the public and government policymakers.*

III. THE MEDIA AND POLITICS

A. AGENDA SETTING

1. The policy agenda consists of issues that attract the serious attention of public officials.
2. The mass media play an important role in drawing public attention to particular issues.

B. CANDIDATE-CENTERED POLITICAL CAMPAIGNS

1. Political campaigns have become more centered on candidates and less focused on issues.
2. The mass media contribute to the candidate-centered campaigns in the following ways:
   - ‣ *By replacing speeches and dialogues with sound bites that average just 7.8 seconds in length.*
   - ‣ *By focusing on day-to-day campaign activities such as rallies, gaffes, scandals, and negative commercials.*
   - ‣ *By engaging in "horse-race journalism," which emphasizes how candidates stand in the polls instead of where they stand on the issues.*

The mass media is an important linkage institution. However, its political role has not been reflected on AP U.S. Government and Politics exams. Of the 360 released multiple-choice questions, less than 10 focused on the mass media. Of the 44 free-response questions asked between 1999 and 2009, just 2 have focused on the mass media. Given this minimal coverage, do not spend too much of your time reviewing the mass media. All of the key points asked thus far are included in this chapter.

Congress

I. A BICAMERAL CONGRESS

A. INTRODUCTION

1. The Framers of the United States Constitution created a bicameral Congress consisting of a House of Representatives and a Senate.
2. The two houses of Congress have different characters.

B. REASONS WHY THE FRAMERS CREATED A BICAMERAL LEGISLATURE

1. Drawing on historical experience
   ▸ *The Framers were intimately familiar with the British system of government.*
   ▸ *The British system featured a bicameral system with a House of Lords and a House of Commons.*
   ▸ *Most of the colonial legislatures and state legislatures were bicameral.*
2. Fulfilling the Connecticut Compromise
   ▸ *Led by Virginia, the large states wanted a bicameral legislature based on population. Led by New Jersey, the small states wanted a unicameral Congress with equal representation for each state.*
   ▸ *The Framers resolved the dispute by agreeing to a compromise calling for a bicameral Congress with representation in a House of Representatives based on population and a Senate in which the states would have equal representation.*

3. Implementing federalism
    ▸ *A bicameral legislature provided for two types of representation. The House represented the interests of the people, while the Senate represented the interests of the states.*
    ▸ *A bicameral legislature fragmented power, thus checking majority interests while protecting minority interests.*
    ▸ *A bicameral legislature slowed the legislative process, thus encouraging careful deliberation and compromise.*

 ## II. DIFFERENCES BETWEEN THE HOUSE AND THE SENATE

A. SIZE, TERMS, AND QUALIFICATIONS

1. House of Representatives
    ▸ *435 members*
    ▸ *Two-year terms*
    ▸ *A representative must be at least 25 years old, an American citizen for 7 years, and a resident of the state from which he or she is elected.*
2. Senate
    ▸ *100 members*
    ▸ *Six-year terms*
    ▸ *A senator must be at least 30 years old, an American citizen for 9 years, and a resident of the state from which he or she is elected.*

B. ELECTION

1. Members of the House of Representatives have always been elected by eligible voters. When the Constitution was ratified, the House of Representatives was the new government's only body directly elected by the people.
2. Senators were originally chosen by state legislatures. The Seventeenth Amendment (1913) mandated that senators be elected by voters in each state.

C. SPECIAL POWERS

1. House of Representatives
    ▸ *Initiates revenue bills*

▸ Brings charges of impeachment against the president,
  vice president, and all civil officers of the United States
▸ Chooses the president when the electoral college is
  deadlocked

2. Senate
   ▸ Ratifies treaties negotiated by the president
   ▸ Possesses the sole power to try or judge impeachment
     cases
   ▸ Confirms judicial appointments, including United States
     attorneys, federal judges, and United States Supreme
     Court justices
   ▸ Confirms executive appointments, including cabinet
     heads, the director of the FBI, and the U.S. attorney
     general

III. THE HOUSE OF REPRESENTATIVES

A. SIZE AND APPORTIONMENT

1. The Constitution does not set the exact size of the House
   of Representatives. It does stipulate that its size shall be
   apportioned or distributed among the states based on their
   respective populations.
2. The Constitution guarantees that each state will have at least
   one representative, regardless of its population. Seven states
   currently have one seat in the House of Representatives.

B. REAPPORTIONMENT

1. The Constitution directs Congress to reapportion (reallocate)
   House seats after a census taken at ten-year intervals.
2. As the population of the United States increased, so did the
   number of representatives in the House. By 1929, the House
   had grown to 435 seats.
3. The Reapportionment Act of 1929 set the permanent size
   of the House at 435 members. As a result, each seat now
   represents an average of 700,000 people.
4. Reapportionment is important because it increases or
   decreases both the number of seats a state has in the House

of Representatives and the number of electoral votes a state has in the electoral college.

5. As a state's representation increases, so does its potential influence. Conversely, as a state's representation decreases, so does its potential influence.

C. DISTRICTS

1. The Constitution does not define or discuss congressional districts.

2. In 1842, Congress stipulated that all seats in the House of Representatives would be filled from single-member districts.

3. The 1842 law assigned each state legislature the responsibility of drawing the boundary lines of its congressional districts.

D. GERRYMANDERING

1. Gerrymandering is the legislative process by which the majority party in each state legislature redraws congressional districts to ensure the maximum number of seats for its candidates.

2. Gerrymandering has the following consequences:
   ▸ *It protects incumbents and discourages challengers.*
   ▸ *It strengthens the majority party while weakening the opposition party.*
   ▸ *It increases or decreases minority representation.*

E. SUPREME COURT LIMITATIONS ON CONGRESSIONAL REDISTRICTING

1. Because rural areas dominated many state legislatures, congressional districts often favored less-populous rural areas of a state.

2. *Wesberry v. Sanders* (1964) set forth the principle of "one person, one vote" in drawing congressional districts. The case triggered widespread redistricting that gave cities and suburbs greater representation in Congress.

3. Supreme Court decisions have placed the following limitations on congressional redistricting:
   ▸ *Districts must be equally populated.*

> ▸ *Districts must be compact. Lines must be contiguous or connected.*
> ▸ *Redistricting cannot dilute minority voting strength.*
> ▸ *District lines cannot be drawn based solely on race. However, race can be one of a variety of factors that are considered.*

4. It is important to note that Supreme Court decisions have not eliminated gerrymandering for partisan political purposes.

IV. CONGRESSIONAL ELECTIONS

A. INCUMBENTS USUALLY WIN

1. During the last 50 years, incumbency has been the single most important factor in determining the outcome of congressional elections.
2. Over 90 percent of House incumbents seeking reelection win.
3. Over 75 percent of Senate incumbents seeking reelection win.

B. REASONS WHY INCUMBENTS WIN

1. Money
   > ▸ *Incumbents are usually able to raise more campaign contributions than their challengers.*
   > ▸ *PACs contribute more money to incumbents than to their challengers.*
   > ▸ *Incumbents outspend challengers by a ratio of more than 2 to 1.*
2. Visibility
   > ▸ *Incumbents are usually better known to the voters than are their challengers.*
   > ▸ *Incumbents have opportunities to participate in highly visible activities that are covered by local newspapers and local television stations.*
3. Constituent service
   > ▸ *There is a close link between constituent service and reelection.*

KEY CONTENT REVIEW

▸ *Members of Congress are able to win supporters by performing casework for their constituents and by bringing home money and jobs ("pork") for their district.*

▸ *Casework consists of helping individual constituents, often by cutting through bureaucratic red tape.*

▸ *Pork is legislation that allows representatives to bring money and jobs to their district. Incumbents often sit on committees that enable them to earmark or designate specific projects for their district. Pork helps representatives earn a reputation for service to their district.*

4. The franking privilege

▸ *The franking privilege refers to the right of members of Congress to mail newsletters to their constituents at the government's expense.*

▸ *Within recent years, members of Congress have extended the franking privilege to include e-mails and recorded phone calls.*

5. Gerrymandering

▸ *Members of the House often represent districts that have been deliberately gerrymandered to include voting blocs that support incumbents.*

▸ *Gerrymandered districts discourage strong challengers from trying to compete with incumbents.*

C. CONSEQUENCES OF THE INCUMBENCY ADVANTAGE

1. Congress contains a large number of experienced leaders, thus enabling it to maintain continuity of leadership and policy.

2. The continuity discourages radical change while encouraging close relations with interest groups.

3. Because incumbents benefit the most from existing campaign finance laws, they have no incentive to reform them.

Test Tip

Polls repeatedly report that a majority of Americans disapprove of the job Congress is doing. Yet the same polls also report that a majority of Americans believe that their own representative deserves to be reelected. The AP U.S. Government and Politics Development Committee has devoted more multiple-choice questions to this paradox than to any other topic. Be sure that you carefully study the reasons why incumbents are usually reelected.

V. HOW CONGRESS IS ORGANIZED

A. THE ROLE OF POLITICAL PARTIES

1. Political parties play a key role in the organization of both houses of Congress.
2. The majority party is the party in each chamber with the most votes.
3. The minority party is the party in each chamber with the second most votes.
4. The majority party enjoys the following advantages:
    - *It holds committee chairs.*
    - *It chooses the Speaker of the House.*
    - *It assigns bills to committees.*
    - *It holds the majority on each committee.*
    - *It controls the House Rules Committee.*
    - *It sets the legislative agenda.*

B. THE HOUSE OF REPRESENTATIVES

1. The House of Representatives has always been much larger than the Senate. As a result, it has a more formal structure and is governed by stricter rules. For example, debate is much more restricted in the House than in the Senate.
2. The Speaker of the House
    - *Presides over the House of Representatives*
    - *Overseas House business*
    - *Stands second in line for presidential succession*
3. Other House leaders
    - *The majority leader is the elected leader of the party that controls the House of Representatives.*
    - *The minority leader is the elected leader of the party with the second-highest number of elected representatives in the House of Representatives.*
    - *Both parties have elected whips who maintain close contact with their members and try to ensure party unity on important votes.*

C. THE SENATE

1. The Senate is smaller and thus less formally organized than the House of Representatives. In contrast to the House, the Senate operates more on informal understandings.

2. The Vice President
    - ▸ *The Constitution makes the vice president the president of the Senate.*
    - ▸ *The vice president may vote only to break a tie.*

3. Other Senate leaders
    - ▸ *The president pro tempore presides over the Senate in the absence of the vice president. The position is held by a member of the majority party with the longest service in the Senate.*
    - ▸ *The majority leader is the elected leader of the party that controls the Senate. The majority leader is the true leader of the Senate.*
    - ▸ *The minority leader is the elected leader of the party with the second-highest number of members in the Senate.*

D. THE COMMITTEE SYSTEM

1. The importance of committees
    - ▸ *Both the House and the Senate are divided into committees.*
    - ▸ *Committees play a dominant role in congressional policymaking.*
    - ▸ *The committee system is particularly important in the House of Representatives.*

2. Standing committees
    - ▸ *Standing committees are permanent bodies that continue from one Congress to the next.*
    - ▸ *They focus on legislation in a particular area, such as foreign relations or agriculture.*
    - ▸ *All bills are referred to standing committees, where they can be amended, passed, or killed.*
    - ▸ *Standing committees foster the development of expertise by their members.*
    - ▸ *Standing committees are divided into subcommittees, where the details of legislation are worked out.*

3. Other types of committees
   ▸ *Select committees are special panels formed for a specific purpose and for a limited time. Select committees are usually formed to conduct an investigation into a current matter of great public concern.*
   ▸ *Joint committees include members of both houses. They are similar in function to select committees and often focus public attention on a major issue.*
   ▸ *Conference committees are temporary bodies that are formed to resolve differences between House and Senate versions of a bill. Members are appointed by the party leadership and are drawn from the House and Senate committees that originally considered the bill.*

E. THE HOUSE RULES COMMITTEE

1. The Rules Committee is controlled by the Speaker. It is often called the "traffic cop" or the Speaker's "right arm."
2. The Rules Committee sets the guidelines for floor debate. It gives each bill a rule that places the bill on the legislative calendar, limits time for debate, and determines the type of amendments that will be allowed.
3. A closed rule sets strict time limits on debates and forbids amendments from the floor.
4. An open rule sets less strict time limits on debate and permits amendments from the floor.

F. THE HOUSE COMMITTEE ON WAYS AND MEANS

1. The committee has jurisdiction on all taxation, tariffs, and other revenue-raising measures.
2. Members of the Ways and Means Committee cannot serve on other House committees.

G. COMMITTEE CHAIRS AND THE SENIORITY SYSTEM

1. Committee chairs exercise great power and enjoy considerable prestige.
   ▸ *They call meetings, schedule hearings, hire staff, recommend majority members to sit on conference committees, and select all subcommittee chairs.*

> ‣ *They often receive favors from lobbyists and contributions from PACs.*

2. Historically, committee chairs were chosen by a seniority system in which the majority party member with the most continuous service on the committee automatically became the chair.

3. Chairs in both the House and Senate are now elected positions. However, seniority is still the norm for selecting chairs in both chambers.

VI. THE LEGISLATIVE PROCESS

A. INTRODUCTION

1. Approximately 5,000 bills are introduced each year.
2. Only about 125, or about 2.5 percent, of these bills are made into law.
3. The bicameral Congress and its complex committee system present a formidable series of legislative obstacles that defeat most bills.
4. The legislative process is lengthy, deliberate, fragmented, and characterized by negotiation and compromise.

B. CREATING BILLS

1. Anyone can write a bill.
2. Most bills are not written by members of Congress.
3. Most bills originate in the executive branch.
4. Business, labor, agriculture, and other interest groups often draft bills.
5. Only members of Congress can introduce bills. They do so, by dropping a bill into the "hopper," a box hanging on the edge of the clerk's desk.

C. COMMITTEE ACTION

1. The House and the Senate have parallel processes.
2. Bills are assigned a number and then sent to an appropriate committee. The bill is usually referred by the committee

chair to a subcommittee for study, hearings, revisions, and approval.

3. Most bills die in committees, where they are pigeonholed or buried.

4. If a majority of the House wishes to consider a bill that has been pigeonholed, the bill can be blasted out of the committee with a discharge petition signed by a majority of the House members.

5. Bills approved by a subcommittee are then returned to the full committee, where members can mark up or add items to the bill.

6. Committees can reject the bill or send it to the House or Senate floor with a positive recommendation.

D. FLOOR ACTION

1. HOUSE OF REPRESENTATIVES
   ▸ *The House Rules Committee gives the bill a rule, placing it on the legislative calendar, allowing a specified time for debate, and determining if any amendments will be allowed.*
   ▸ *The bill is debated and a vote is ultimately taken by the full House.*

2. SENATE
   ▸ *Unlike the House, Senate procedures permit members to speak on the floor as long as they wish.*
   ▸ *A filibuster is a way of delaying or preventing action on a bill by using long speeches and unlimited debate to "talk a bill to death."*
   ▸ *Filibusters can be stopped only if 60 senators vote for cloture to cut off debate.*
   ▸ *Filibusters are so successful that important bills no longer require a simple majority of 51 votes to pass. Instead, supporters need a 60-vote majority so that they can invoke cloture to end a filibuster and then pass their bill.*
   ▸ *In addition to threatening to filibuster, a senator can ask to be informed before a particular bill is brought to the floor. Known as a hold, this parliamentary procedure stops a bill from coming to the floor until the hold is removed.*

> ▸ *If a bill overcomes these obstacles, it will ultimately be voted up or down by the full Senate.*

E. CONFERENCE ACTION

1. If a bill is passed in different versions by the House and the Senate, a conference committee will be formed to work out the differences. The conference committee is comprised of members from the original House and Senate committees.
2. The conference committee bill is then returned to each chamber for a vote.

F. HOW MEMBERS VOTE

1. In the instructed delegate model, members of Congress cast votes that reflect the preferences of the majority of their constituents.
2. In the trustee model, members of Congress use their best judgment to make policy in the interests of the people.
3. In the politico model, members of Congress act as delegates or trustees depending on the issue.

VII. CONGRESS AND THE EXECUTIVE BRANCH

A. OVERSIGHT

1. Oversight refers to congressional review of the activities of an executive agency, department, or office.
2. The Senate exercises a special oversight function by confirming cabinet heads and presidential appointments to the federal courts.
3. Methods of congressional oversight include:
    - ▸ *Setting guidelines for new agencies*
    - ▸ *Holding hearings and conducting investigations*
    - ▸ *Using budget control*
    - ▸ *Reorganizing an agency*
    - ▸ *Evaluating an agency's programs*

B. FOREIGN POLICY

1. The constitutional division of power
   - ▸ *Congress has the power to declare war. The Senate has the power to ratify treaties.*
   - ▸ *The president is the commander-in-chief and has the power to wage war. In addition, the president has the power to negotiate treaties.*

2. The War Powers Resolution
   - ▸ *Passed by Congress in 1973, the War Powers Resolution was a response to presidential actions during the Vietnam War. The resolution was designed to ensure that Congress had a greater voice in presidential decisions committing military forces to hostile situations overseas.*
   - ▸ *The War Powers Resolution requires the president to notify Congress within 48 hours of deploying troops. The president must bring troops home from hostilities within 60 to 90 days unless Congress extends the time.*

Test Tip

Do not overlook the War Powers Resolution. Most released exams have had a multiple-choice question on this topic. In addition, the War Powers Resolution was featured in a free-response question asked in 2007.

KEY CONTENT REVIEW

Presidential Elections and the Presidency

I. THE ROAD TO THE PRESIDENCY

A. THE PRESIDENTIAL PRIMARIES

1. In the early 1800s, congressional leaders held a caucus to select presidential candidates.

2. Supporters of Andrew Jackson criticized the caucus system for being elitist. During the 1830s, the Jackson Democrats and the Whigs held party conventions to nominate their presidential candidates.

3. Party bosses soon dominated the conventions. During the early 1900s, Progressive reformers promoted primary elections as a way of giving voters a greater role in the nomination process.

4. In 2008, 40 states held presidential primaries. The first primary is traditionally held in New Hampshire. In a process called frontloading, three-fourths of the primaries are now held between February and mid-March.

5. Primaries can be closed or open:

   ▸ *In a closed primary, voters are required to identify a party preference before the election and are not allowed to split their ticket.*

   ▸ *In an open primary, voters can decide on Election Day whether they want to participate in the Democratic or Republican contest.*

6. In the past, most presidential primaries were winner-take-all elections in which the candidate with the most votes won all the delegates. The Democratic Party has now replaced winner-take-all primaries with a proportional system that awards delegates based on the percentage of votes a

candidate receives. The Republican Party currently uses both winner-take-all and proportional representation elections.

7. Some states use a complex system of local caucuses and district conventions to select delegates. Iowa holds the best known and most influential caucus.

8. Critics argue that candidates devote too much time to Iowa and New Hampshire. Although both states are relatively small, they play a crucial role in generating media attention.

9. Only about 25 percent of adult citizens cast ballots in primary elections. Primary voters tend to be party activists who are older and more affluent than voters in the general election.

B. THE PARTY CONVENTIONS

1. In the past, party conventions selected their presidential and vice-presidential candidates after days of tense and often dramatic bargaining. As a result of victories in the primaries and caucuses, the leading contender now almost always has the nomination locked up before the convention begins.

2. The conventions now serve three major functions:
   ‣ *They formally name the party's presidential and vice-presidential candidates.*
   ‣ *They adopt a party platform.*
   ‣ *They attempt to unify the party and generate positive publicity and momentum.*

C. CAMPAIGN SPENDING AND REFORM

1. Campaign costs have skyrocketed. In 1988, George Bush and Michael Dukakis spent a combined total of $60.3 million to fund their activities during the primary season. In 2008, Barack Obama and John McCain spent $408 million to fund their primary campaigns.

2. The Federal Election Reform Act of 1974
   ‣ *Created a Federal Election Commission to administer and enforce campaign finance laws.*
   ‣ *Provided partial public funding for presidential primaries.*
   ‣ *Provided full public financing for major party candidates in the general election.*
   ‣ *Placed limitations on individual contributions to presidential candidates.*

3. *Buckley v. Valeo* (1976)
   ▸ *The Supreme Court struck down the portion of the Federal Election Reform Act that limited the amount of money an individual could contribute to his or her own campaign.*
   ▸ *The Court ruled that contributing to one's own campaign is a form of protected free speech: "The candidate, no less than any other person, has a First Amendment right to engage in the discussion of public issues and vigorously and tirelessly to advocate his own election."*

4. Soft money
   ▸ *Soft money includes unregulated donations to political parties for party-building expenses such as grassroots activities and generic party advertising.*
   ▸ *Reform laws failed to regulate soft money donations.*
   ▸ *Soft money was often used to circumvent limitations on hard money contributions.*

5. The Bipartisan Campaign Reform Act of 2002
   ▸ *Reformers led by Senators John McCain and Russell Feingold aimed to eliminate soft money contributions.*
   ▸ *The Bipartisan Campaign Reform Act of 2002 banned soft money contributions.*

6. 527 groups
   ▸ *A 527 group is a tax-exempt organization created to influence the political process.*
   ▸ *527 groups are not regulated by the Federal Election Commission because they do not coordinate their activities with a candidate or party.*
   ▸ *In 2004, 527 groups spent over $420 million on political messages.*

D. THE ELECTORAL COLLEGE

1. Introduction
   ▸ *The Framers created the electoral college to safeguard the presidency from direct popular election.*
   ▸ *Each state has as many electoral votes as its combined total of representatives and senators. In the 2008 presidential election, seven states and the District of Columbia had three electoral votes, while California had 55 electoral votes.*

KEY CONTENT REVIEW

▸ *Electors were originally chosen by the state legislatures. Today, they are selected by the parties. Although the Framers expected electors to be independent, they are now expected to vote for their party's candidates for president and vice president.*

2. Consequences of the winner-take-all electoral college

▸ *The electoral college is a winner-take-all system. The presidential candidate who receives the most votes wins all of a state's electoral votes.*

▸ *Candidates devote a disproportionate amount of time and resources to closely contested states, swing states, and competitive states.*

▸ *Candidates emphasize issues that may swing a key bloc of voters in a pivotal state. For example, candidates appeal to Florida's large bloc of Cuban American voters by stressing their opposition to Fidel Castro.*

▸ *The winner-take-all system severely restricts the prospects of third-party candidates.*

3. Reasons why the electoral college has not been abolished

▸ *It would require a constitutional amendment to abolish the electoral college.*

▸ *The electoral college collectively benefits the small states that are guaranteed at least 3 electoral votes.*

▸ *The electoral college benefits racial minorities and interest groups located in key states.*

▸ *There is no consensus on how to reform the electoral college.*

II. THE PRESIDENT AS CHIEF EXECUTIVE

A. EXECUTIVE POWER

1. The Constitution declares that "the executive Power shall be vested in a President of the United States of America."

2. As the nation's chief executive, the president enforces the provisions of federal laws and administers a vast federal bureaucracy that spends more than $3 trillion a year and includes 2.7 million civilian employees.

B. APPOINTMENT POWER

1. The president has the power to appoint all of the following top-ranking officers of the federal government:
   - ▸ *Cabinet members and their top aides.*
   - ▸ *The heads of independent agencies.*
   - ▸ *Ambassadors and other diplomats.*
   - ▸ *All federal judges, U.S. marshals, and attorneys.*

2. These appointments are all subject to confirmation by a majority of the Senate.

3. The president's appointment power is limited by an unwritten rule known as senatorial courtesy. According to this custom, the Senate will not approve a presidential appointment opposed by a majority party senator from the state in which the appointee would serve.

C. REMOVAL POWER

1. Presidents have the power to dismiss most of the officials he or she appoints.

2. It is important to note that the president cannot dismiss federal judges or commissioners of independent regulatory agencies.

D. THE CABINET

1. The cabinet currently includes 14 executive department heads and the attorney general. These 15 executive departments employ nearly two-thirds of the federal government's civilian employees.

2. Cabinet members often have divided loyalties. Their loyalty to the president can be undermined by loyalty to the institutional goals of their own department.

3. The following factors explain why presidents often experience difficulty in controlling cabinet departments:
   - ▸ *Interest groups often form close ties with cabinet departments.*
   - ▸ *The careers of many civil servants extend beyond a single presidential administration. As a result, they develop a strong loyalty to their department.*

▸ *Congress competes with the president for influence over cabinet departments.*

E. THE EXECUTIVE OFFICE OF THE PRESIDENT

1. The Office of Management and Budget (OMB)
   ▸ *The OMB is the largest office within the Executive Office of the President. It includes a staff of over 500 career officials.*
   ▸ *The OMB's primary responsibility is to assist the president in overseeing the preparation of the federal budget.*

2. The National Security Council (NSC)
   ▸ *The NSC is composed of the president's principal foreign and military advisers. It includes the vice president, secretary of state, secretary of the treasury, secretary of defense, national security advisor, and others as necessary.*
   ▸ *The NSC's principal function is to advise and assist the president on national security and foreign policies.*

3. The Council of Economic Advisors (CEA)
   ▸ *The CEA is a group of three leading economists who advise the president on economic policy.*
   ▸ *The CEA prepares the annual* Economic Report of the President.

F. THE WHITE HOUSE STAFF

1. The White House staff includes key presidential aides such as the chief of staff and the press secretary.

2. The chief of staff is the highest-ranking member of the Executive Office of the President. The chief of staff's duties include selecting and supervising key White House staff and managing the flow of people and information into the Oval Office.

3. The White House staff must be personally loyal to the president.

4. The president can appoint and dismiss members of the White House staff without Senate approval.

5. The White House staff's primary responsibility is to provide the president with policy options and analysis.

III. THE PRESIDENT AS CHIEF LEGISLATOR

A. LEGISLATIVE POWERS

1. The Constitution does not actually call the president the chief legislator.
2. The Constitution does give the president the following powers:
   ▸ *The president is required to give a State of the Union address to Congress.*
   ▸ *The president can bring issues to the attention of Congress "from time to time."*
   ▸ *The president can veto congressional legislation.*
3. Presidents use their roles as national leader and head of the party to set the policy agenda. As a result, the president now initiates much of the major legislation that Congress considers. As noted by one prominent political scientist, "[N]o other single actor in the political system has quite the capability of the President to set agendas."

B. THE VETO POWER

1. Presidential options
   ▸ *The president can sign a bill into law.*
   ▸ *The president can veto a bill. Congress may override the veto with a two-thirds vote in each chamber.*
   ▸ *The president can wait ten full days. If Congress is still in session, the bill will become law without the president's signature.*
   ▸ *The president can exercise a pocket veto by waiting ten full days. If Congress adjourns before the ten days are up, the bill will die.*
2. Using the veto
   ▸ *Congress is usually unable to override a presidential veto. Less than 10 percent of presidential vetoes have been overridden.*
   ▸ *Presidents often use the threat of a veto to persuade Congress to modify a bill.*
   ▸ *A vetoed bill is often revised and then passed in another form.*

  ‣ *Congress often inserts provisions the president wants into an objectionable bill in order to reduce the chances of a veto.*

3. The line-item veto
  ‣ *The president must accept or reject an entire bill. He or she cannot veto a portion of a bill.*
  ‣ *Many state governors have a line-item veto that allows them to veto specific items in a bill.*
  ‣ *In 1996, Congress passed a Line-Item Veto Act giving the president the power to strike individual items from major appropriations bills. Supporters hoped the line-item veto would enable the president to reduce wasteful government spending, pork, and earmarks.*
  ‣ *Just two years later, the Supreme Court struck down the line-item veto as an unconstitutional expansion of the president's veto power.*
  ‣ *A line-item veto can be enacted only by a constitutional amendment.*

C. WORKING WITH CONGRESS

1. Presidents prefer to establish a cooperative bipartisan relationship with Congress.
2. Presidents use the following strategies to influence Congress to pass legislation:
  ‣ *Assigning legislative liaisons from the Executive Office of the President to lobby legislators.*
  ‣ *Working with both the majority and the minority leaders.*
  ‣ *Using the media to focus public attention on important issues.*
  ‣ *Using high presidential approval ratings to persuade legislators to support presidential programs.*
  ‣ *Bargaining with wavering legislators by offering concessions and pork that will benefit a member's district.*

D. DIVIDED GOVERNMENT

1. Divided government occurs when the presidency and Congress are controlled by different parties. It also occurs

when the chambers of Congress are controlled by different parties.

2. Divided government has been a frequent result of elections over the past half century.

3. The pattern of divided government has had a number of important consequences:
   ▸ *It has heightened partisanship and made it more difficult for moderates to negotiate compromises.*
   ▸ *It has slowed the legislative process and thus created gridlock.*
   ▸ *It has contributed to the decline of public trust in government.*

4. Divided government poses particular problems for the president in making federal appointments. It fosters stricter committee scrutiny, narrows the field of potential candidates, and sometimes sparks character attacks on nominees.

5. Presidents attempt to overcome the problem of divided government by using the following strategies:
   ▸ *Using the media to generate public support.*
   ▸ *Threatening to veto objectionable legislation.*
   ▸ *Making deals with key congressional leaders.*
   ▸ *Building coalitions with key interest groups.*
   ▸ *Increasing reliance on the White House staff.*

Divided government has been a persistent fact of political life for the past half century. A number of free-response questions have asked to explain the impact of divided government on public policy, legislative gridlock, and federal appointments.

IV. THE PRESIDENT AND NATIONAL SECURITY

A. FORMAL CONSTITUTIONAL POWERS

1. The president is the commander-in-chief and thus has the power to deploy troops.

2. The president appoints all ambassadors subject to Senate confirmation.

3. The president negotiates treaties, which are then subject to Senate ratification.

4. The president has the sole power to recognize nations.

5. The president receives ambassadors and other public ministers.

B. INFORMAL POWERS

1. The president can negotiate executive agreements with the heads of foreign governments.

2. The president is a recognized global leader who meets with world leaders to build international coalitions.

3. The president is expected to manage international crises.

4. The president has access to confidential information that is not available to Congress or the public.

C. THE PRESIDENT AS CHIEF DIPLOMAT

1. The president's role as chief diplomat is derived from delegated powers stated in the Constitution. Congress normally defers to the president in foreign affairs.

2. The president can both extend diplomatic relations to foreign governments and also terminate relations with other nations. For example, President Carter recognized the People's Republic of China and severed relations with Iran.

3. The president has the sole power to negotiate treaties with other nations. For example, President Wilson negotiated the Treaty of Versailles, which ended World War I, and President Carter negotiated the Panama Canal Treaty, which returned the Panama Canal to Panama. The Constitution gives the Senate the power to approve or reject treaties by a two-thirds vote. The Senate rejected the Treaty of Versailles and approved the Panama Canal Treaty.

4. Presidents rely more and more on executive agreements rather than formal treaties. An executive agreement is a pact between the president and a head of a foreign state. Executive agreements do not have to be approved by the Senate. Unlike treaties, executive agreements are not part

of American law and are not binding on future presidents. Notable examples of executive agreements include the destroyers-for-bases deal with Great Britain, the Vietnam peace agreement, and the SALT I agreement limiting offensive nuclear weapons.

D. THE PRESIDENT AS COMMANDER-IN-CHIEF

1. The Constitution specifically makes the president the commander-in-chief of America's armed forces.
2. The Constitution specifically grants Congress the power to declare war. Nonetheless, since World War II, modern presidents have frequently sent U.S. forces into combat without a formal declaration of war. Examples include the Korean War, the Vietnam War, the Persian Gulf War, and the Iraq War.
3. The president's commitment of troops into battle has generated great controversy between the executive and legislative branches.
4. In 1973, Congress passed the War Powers Resolution to ensure congressional involvement in decisions committing military forces to hostile situations overseas. The War Powers Resolution includes the following key provisions:
   ▸ *The president must notify Congress within 48 hours of deploying troops.*
   ▸ *The president must bring troops home from hostilities within 60 to 90 days unless Congress extends the time.*

V. THE PRESIDENT'S JUDICIAL POWERS

A. GRANTING REPRIEVES AND PARDONS

1. The Constitution gives the president the power to grant reprieves and pardons.
2. A reprieve is the postponement of the execution of a sentence.
3. A pardon is the legal forgiveness of a crime. For example, in 1974, President Ford pardoned former president Nixon for crimes he committed during the Watergate scandal.

KEY CONTENT REVIEW

B. APPOINTING SUPREME COURT JUSTICES

1. The president has the power to appoint justices to the Supreme Court. Presidential nominees must be confirmed by the Senate.
2. Presidents use this power to select justices with judicial philosophies that are compatible with their interpretation of constitutional questions.

VI. THE PRESIDENT AND THE MEDIA

A. THE IMPORTANCE OF PUBLIC SUPPORT

1. Public support is critical to presidential success.
2. One top aide to President Reagan underscored the importance of public support when he said, "Everything here is built on the idea that the President's success depends on grassroots support."

B. PRESIDENTIAL APPROVAL LEVELS

1. For over 50 years, the Gallup Poll has asked Americans, "Do you approve or disapprove of the way [name of the President] is handling his job as president?"
2. Data from the Gallup Poll and other public opinion surveys show that the following factors increase presidential approval ratings:
   - *Brief "honeymoon" periods at the beginning of an administration.*
   - *Positive media coverage of presidential activities and decisions.*
   - *Foreign policy successes.*
   - *Foreign crises that produce a "rally round the flag" effect.*
   - *Strong economic growth and low unemployment.*
3. Data from the Gallup Poll and other public opinion surveys show that the following factors decrease presidential approval ratings:
   - *Scandals involving the president and/or top aides.*
   - *A gap between high expectations and poor job performance.*

‣ *Foreign wars that go badly over a protracted period of time.*

‣ *Weak economic growth and high unemployment.*

C. THE PRESIDENT AND THE MEDIA

1. The media plays a key role in influencing how the public perceives the president.

2. The president is generally more successful than congressional leaders in using the media to set the policy agenda.

3. The following factors give the president an advantage over Congress in gaining media attention:

   ‣ *The president represents the entire nation. In contrast, members of Congress represent districts and/or states.*

   ‣ *The president is the leader of the "free world."*

   ‣ *The president is more powerful than any individual member of Congress.*

   ‣ *The president speaks with a single voice. In contrast, Congress has 535 competing members.*

*Most AP U.S. Government and Politics exams contain a multiple-choice question asking you to identify which answer choice is **not** a presidential role or formal power. It is important to remember that the Constitution does not allow the president to form new cabinet-level departments, raise revenue, or declare war. While the president is the leader of his or her political party, this role is not authorized by the Constitution.*

KEY CONTENT REVIEW

The Federal Bureaucracy

I. THE BUREAUCRACY

A. KEY DEFINITIONS AND FACTS

1. A bureaucracy is a large, complex organization of appointed officials.
2. The federal bureaucracy includes all of the agencies, people, and procedures through which the federal government operates.
   - ▸ *There are approximately 2.7 million civilian and 1.4 million military federal government employees.*
   - ▸ *Half of all the civilian federal employees work for the Department of Defense and an additional 28 percent work for the Postal Service.*

B. KEY FEATURES OF A BUREAUCRACY

1. Hierarchical authority—a chain of command in which authority follows from the top down.
2. Job specialization—each employee has defined duties and responsibilities.
3. Formal rules—all employees must follow established procedures and regulations.

II. THE GROWTH OF THE FEDERAL BUREAUCRACY

A. THE SPOILS SYSTEM

1. The federal bureaucracy was originally drawn from an elite group of upper-class white males.

2. Proclaiming "to the victor belong the spoils," Andrew Jackson awarded federal posts to party loyalists.

B. THE CIVIL SERVICE

1. The Pendleton Act (1883) created the federal civil service. In a civil service system, workers are selected according to merit, not party loyalty.
2. The Office of Personnel Management (OPM)
   - ▸ *Administers civil service laws and regulations.*
   - ▸ *Is in charge of hiring for most federal agencies.*

C. FEDERAL AND STATE EMPLOYEES

1. Federal government employees currently account for 3 percent of all civilian jobs.
2. The number of federal government employees has remained constant since 1950.
3. The number of state and local government employees has steadily increased since 1950.
4. Block grants have contributed to the widening gap between the number of federal and state employees by shifting resources from the federal government to state and local governments.
5. Federal mandates have also shifted more responsibility to states, causing an increase in the number of their public employees.

III. THE FEDERAL BUREAUCRACY: ORGANIZATION AND KEY FUNCTIONS

A. THE CABINET DEPARTMENTS

1. There are 15 cabinet departments. With the exception of the Department of Justice (headed by the attorney general), each department is headed by a secretary.
2. All 15 heads are chosen by the president and approved by the Senate.
3. The Treasury Department has authority over the printing of currency.

4. Cabinet secretaries often develop a strong loyalty to their departments. As a result, cabinet members are often not close presidential advisors.

B. THE INDEPENDENT REGULATORY AGENCIES

1. Created to protect the public by regulating key sectors of the economy.
2. The Interstate Commerce Commission (ICC), Securities and Exchange Commission (SEC), National Labor Relations Board (NLRB), and the Federal Reserve Board (FRB) are among the best-known independent regulatory agencies.
3. The independent regulatory agencies are led by small commissions appointed by the president and confirmed by the Senate. Note that the commissioners cannot be removed by the president during their terms of office.
4. The Federal Reserve Board
   ▸ *The Federal Reserve Board's primary responsibility is to set monetary policy.*
   ▸ *Monetary policy includes setting bank interest rates, controlling inflation, regulating the money supply, and adjusting bank reserve requirements.*
   ▸ *The Federal Reserve Board has great independence. This freedom removes monetary policy from politics. As a result, the Federal Reserve Board is usually able to use its economic expertise to develop monetary policies without undue interference from political parties and interest groups.*

Test Tip

Be sure you know the difference between monetary policy and fiscal policy. Monetary policy refers to the money supply and interest rates. The Federal Reserve Board has the primary responsibility for monetary policy. Fiscal policy refers to taxing and spending policies. Both the executive and legislative branches share responsibility for fiscal policies.

C. THE GOVERNMENT CORPORATIONS

1. Government corporations provide a service that could be provided by the private sector.

2. The Corporation for Public Broadcasting, the Tennessee Valley Authority, Amtrak, and the U.S. Postal Service are the best known government corporations.

D. INDEPENDENT EXECUTIVE AGENCIES

1. The independent executive agencies include most of the non-cabinet departments.
2. The National Aeronautics and Space Administration (NASA), the National Science Foundation (NSF), the Environmental Protection Agency (EPA), and the Government Services Administration (GSA) are the best known independent executive agencies.

IV. IMPLEMENTATION AND REGULATION

A. IMPLEMENTATION

1. Implementation is the translation of policy goals into rules and standard operating procedures.
2. Implementation can break down for a number of reasons, including conflicting goals, a faulty program design, a lack of financial resources, and the fragmentation of responsibilities. For example, prior to the formation of the Office of Homeland Security in 2001, forty-six federal agencies were involved in counterterrorism efforts.
3. Congress usually provides federal agencies with general mandates. As a result, the agencies often have administrative discretion to set specific guidelines for a given problem or situation.

B. REGULATION

1. Regulation is the use of governmental authority to control or change practices in the private sector.
2. The Supreme Court first upheld the right of government to regulate businesses in *Munn v. Illinois* (1877).
3. During the administrations of presidents Reagan and George W. Bush, the federal government deregulated or lifted a

number of restrictions on business. For example, in 1984, Congress disbanded the Civil Aeronautics Board (CAB).

V. THE PRESIDENT AND THE BUREAUCRACY

A. APPOINTMENTS

1. Presidents have the power to appoint senior agency heads and subheads. This enables the president to exercise influence over an agency.
2. The president's power is limited. The Senate has the power to approve the president's appointments. In addition, agency heads often develop a strong loyalty to their departments and thus do not aggressively pursue a president's policy agenda.

B. EXECUTIVE ORDERS

1. An executive order is a directive, order, or regulation issued by the president.
2. Executive orders are based on constitutional or statutory authority and have the force of law.

C. ECONOMIC POWERS

1. The president may use the Office of Management and Budget to cut or add to an agency's budget.
2. It is important to remember that Congress has the sole power to appropriate funds to an agency.

VI. CONGRESS AND THE BUREAUCRACY

A. DIVIDED AUTHORITY

1. The United States has a system of divided supervision in which both the president and Congress exercise authority over the federal bureaucracy.
2. The system of divided supervision creates checks and balances while at the same time often encouraging agencies to play one branch of government against the other.

KEY CONTENT REVIEW

B. OVERSIGHT

1. Congress has the responsibility to exercise legislative oversight over the federal bureaucracy.
2. Congress uses the following methods to oversee the federal bureaucracy:
   ▸ *Exercising budgetary control by setting aside funds for each agency.*
   ▸ *Holding hearings and conducting investigations.*
   ▸ *Reorganizing an agency.*
   ▸ *Setting new guidelines for an agency.*
   ▸ *Spreading out responsibilities in order to prevent any one agency from becoming too powerful.*

VII. INTEREST GROUPS AND THE BUREAUCRACY

A. IRON TRIANGLES

1. An iron triangle is an alliance among an administrative agency, an interest group, and a congressional committee. Each member of the iron triangle provides key services, information, or policy for the others.
2. Iron triangles are so pervasive and powerful that they are often called subgovernments.

B. ISSUE NETWORKS

1. An issue network includes policy experts, media pundits, congressional staffs, and interest groups who regularly debate an issue.
2. The president often fills agency positions with people from an issue network who support his or her views.

Test Tip

Be sure that you know the difference between an iron triangle and an issue network. An iron triangle has three interlocking points—an administrative agency, an interest group, and a congressional committee. An issue network consists of a wide range of people who debate major public policies.

The Federal Court System

I. CHARACTERISTICS OF THE FEDERAL COURT SYSTEM

A. ADVERSARIAL

1. A court provides an arena for two parties to bring their conflicts before an impartial arbiter, or judge.
2. The plaintiff brings a charge.
3. The defendant is the one being charged.

B. PASSIVE

1. Federal judges are restrained by the Constitution to deciding actual disputes or cases rather than hypothetical ones.
2. The judiciary is thus a passive branch of government that depends on others to take the initiative.

C. JURISDICTION

1. Jurisdiction is a court's authority to hear a case.
2. Types of jurisdiction
   ▸ *Original jurisdiction—courts in which a case is first heard.*
   ▸ *Appellate jurisdiction—courts that hear cases brought to them on appeal from a lower court.*
   ▸ *Exclusive jurisdiction—cases that can be heard only in certain courts.*
   ▸ *Concurrent jurisdiction—cases that can be heard in either a federal or a state court.*

D. A COMPLEX DUAL COURT SYSTEM

1. Because of its federal system, the United States has two separate court systems.
2. Each of the 50 states has its own system of courts. Over 97 percent of all criminal cases are heard in state and local courts.
3. The federal judiciary system spans the entire country.

II. THE FEDERAL COURT SYSTEM

A. THE CONSTITUTION

1. The Supreme Court is the only court specifically mentioned in the Constitution.
2. The Constitution gives Congress the power to create all other federal courts.

B. THE JUDICIARY ACT OF 1789

1. The Judiciary Act of 1789 established the basic three-tiered structure of federal courts that still exists.
2. The Judiciary Act of 1789 set the size of the Supreme Court at six justices. This was later expanded to nine in 1869.

C. DISTRICT COURTS

1. There are currently 94 district courts staffed by just under 700 judges. Every state has at least one district court.
2. The district courts handle over 300,000 cases a year, or about 80 percent of the federal caseload.
3. Most cases end in a plea bargain negotiated by the defense and prosecution. Only about 2 percent of the cases are decided by trials.

D. THE COURTS OF APPEALS

1. The courts of appeals are appellate courts authorized to review all district court decisions. In addition, they are empowered to rule on decisions of federal regulatory agencies such as the Federal Trade Commission.

2. The courts of appeals do not hold trials or hear testimony.

E. THE SUPREME COURT

1. The Supreme Court is America's "court of last resort." It reviews cases from the United States courts of appeals and state supreme courts.
2. The Supreme Court is the final arbiter of the Constitution. Supreme Court decisions establish precedents that are binding on the entire nation.
3. *Marbury v. Madison* and judicial review:
    ▸ *The Supreme Court established the power of judicial review in the case of* Marbury v. Madison.
    ▸ *Judicial review is the power of the Supreme Court to declare federal legislation invalid if the legislation violates the Constitution.*

III. THE SELECTION OF JUDGES

A. THE LOWER COURTS

1. All federal judges are appointed by the president and confirmed by a majority vote of the Senate.
2. Senatorial courtesy is an unwritten tradition whereby the Senate will not confirm nominations for lower court positions that are opposed by a senator of the president's own party from the state in which the nominee is to serve.

B. THE SUPREME COURT

1. Nomination criteria
    ▸ *Competence—Nominees are expected to have impressive credentials, including prior judicial or governmental experience.*
    ▸ *Ideology and policy preferences—Nominees are expected to share the president's policy preferences. For example, Franklin Delano Roosevelt appointed justices who supported his New Deal programs, while Ronald Reagan appointed justices who were sympathetic to his conservative goals.*

> ▸ *Race, ethnicity, and gender—Contemporary presidents pay close attention to race, ethnicity, and gender. The Supreme Court has had two African American justices, three female justices, and one Hispanic justice. Sonia Sotomayor is the Court's 111th justice, its third female justice, and its first Hispanic justice.*

2. The confirmation process

> ▸ *The names of possible nominees are sent to the Federal Bureau of Investigation for a thorough background check. In addition, the names of nominees are usually sent to the American Bar Association (ABA) for a professional rating.*
> ▸ *Interest groups are playing an increasingly important role in the confirmation process. Interest group tactics include public protest demonstrations, appearances on TV and radio talk shows, media advertisements, editorials, and e-mails to senators.*
> ▸ *The Senate Judiciary Committee holds public hearings on each Supreme Court nominee. The committee then makes a recommendation to the full Senate.*

IV. HOW THE SUPREME COURT WORKS

A. SELECTING CASES

1. The Supreme Court exercises original jurisdiction in cases involving the following:

> ▸ *Two or more states.*
> ▸ *The United States and a state government.*
> ▸ *The United States and foreign ambassadors and diplomats.*

2. Writs of *certiorari*

> ▸ *The Court's original jurisdiction only generates two to three cases a year. The remaining cases come under the Court's appellate jurisdiction.*
> ▸ *Nearly all appellate cases now reach the Supreme Court by a writ of* certiorari. *A writ of* certiorari *is an order by the Court directing a lower court to send up the record in a given case for its review.*

> ▸ *The* certiorari *process enables the Supreme Court to control its own caseload. Cases must involve a serious constitutional issue or the interpretation of a federal statute, action, or treaty.*

3. The Rule of Four

> ▸ *Supreme Court clerks screen the approximately 9,000 petitions that come to the Supreme Court each term. The clerks are exceptional law school graduates who usually have experience clerking for a judge on one of the courts of appeal.*
> ▸ *The justices conduct weekly conference meetings where they discuss petitions prepared by their clerks.*
> ▸ *For a case to be heard on appeal, at least four of the nine justices must agree to hear the case. This is called the Rule of Four.*

Test Tip

The Supreme Court agrees to hear very few lower court appeals. Be sure that you can identify a writ of certiorari and the Rule of Four and explain their role in the case selection process.

4. The solicitor general

> ▸ *The solicitor general is the fourth-ranking member of the Department of Justice.*
> ▸ *The solicitor general is responsible for handling all appeals on behalf of the United States government to the Supreme Court.*
> ▸ *The solicitor general plays an important role in influencing the Court's decision on which cases to hear.*

B. FILING BRIEFS

1. Each party is required to file a brief, or detailed written statement, arguing one side of a case. Briefs cite relevant facts, legal principles, and precedents that support their arguments.

2. Interested persons and groups that are not actual parties to the case may file *amicus curiae* ("friend of the court") briefs. Cases involving controversial issues such as affirmative action

and abortion attract a large number of *amicus curiae* briefs. Interest groups use *amicus curiae* briefs to lobby the Court.

C. LISTENING TO ORAL ARGUMENTS

1. Oral arguments are open to the public.
2. Attorneys are allowed exactly 30 minutes to present their case.

D. DISCUSSION AND VOTING

1. The justices discuss each case in a closed meeting held on Friday.
2. The Chief Justice presides over the meeting. Chief Justice Roberts is known to encourage discussion.

E. WRITING OPINIONS

1. After reaching a decision, the justices must write a formal opinion. Opinions present the issues, establish precedents, and set guidelines for lower courts.
2. Types of opinions
   ▸ *Majority opinion—Officially known as "the opinion of the Court," the majority opinion is the law of the land.*
   ▸ *Concurring opinion—Supports the majority opinion but stresses different constitutional or legal reasons for reaching the judgment.*
   ▸ *Minority or dissenting opinion—Expresses a point of view that disagrees with the majority opinion. Dissenting opinions have no legal standing.*

V. FACTORS THAT INFLUENCE SUPREME COURT DECISIONS

A. PRECEDENT

1. *Stare decisis*
   ▸ Stare decisis *is a Latin phrase meaning "let the decision stand."*

> ▸ *The vast majority of Supreme Court decisions are based on precedents established in earlier cases.*
> ▸ *Precedents help make Supreme Court decisions more uniform, predictable, and efficient.*

2. Examples
> ▸ *In* Marbury v. Madison, *the Court established the principle of judicial review as applied to Congress and the president. In* Martin v. Hunter's Lessee, *the Court extended the power of judicial review to overrule state courts.*
> ▸ *In* Baker v. Carr, *the Supreme Court established the principle of one person, one vote. In* Wesberry v. Sanders, *the Court applied this principle to congressional districts.*

3. Exceptions
> ▸ *Although precedent is very important, the Court can overturn previous decisions.*
> ▸ *For example,* Plessy v. Ferguson *permitted segregation if the facilities were "separate but equal." The Court reversed this ruling in* Brown v. Board of Education of Topeka, *declaring that "segregation is a denial of the equal protection of the laws."*

B. JUDICIAL PHILOSOPHY

1. Judicial restraint
> ▸ *Advocates of judicial restraint argue that the Supreme Court should use precedent and the Framers' original intent to decide cases.*
> ▸ *Advocates of judicial restraint also argue that the Supreme Court should defer to the elected institutions of government.*

2. Judicial activism
> ▸ *Advocates of judicial activism argue that the federal courts must correct injustices when other branches of government or the states refuse to do so.*
> ▸ *Advocates of judicial activism point to the Court's decision in* Brown v. Board of Education of Topeka *as an example of how judicial activism promoted social justice.*

C. PUBLIC OPINION

1. The Constitution insulated Supreme Court justices from direct political pressures.
   - ▸ *Justices are appointed to serve life terms subject only to good behavior.*
   - ▸ *The salaries of justices cannot be reduced.*
   - ▸ *The* certiorari *process enables the Supreme Court to set its own agenda.*
   - ▸ *The public has limited access to Court proceedings.*

2. The Supreme Court is nonetheless aware of and sensitive to public opinion.
   - ▸ *The appointment and confirmation processes keep the Supreme Court from deviating too far from public opinion.*
   - ▸ *Congress and the state legislatures can amend the Constitution.*
   - ▸ *Congress can change the Supreme Court's appellate jurisdiction.*
   - ▸ *Congress has the power to change the number of justices on the Court.*
   - ▸ *Justices can be impeached.*

Test Tip

Judicial restraint and judicial activism are well-known philosophies that appear on most AP U.S. Government and Politics exams. Do not overlook the ways in which the Supreme Court is insulated from public opinion and the factors that restrain the Court from straying too far from public opinion.

The Federal Budget and Social Security

 I. **INTRODUCTION**

A. KEY TERMS

1. Budget
   - ▸ *A financial plan for the use of money, personnel, and property.*
   - ▸ *The federal budget for 2010 is $3.6 trillion.*
2. Balanced budget
   - ▸ *When expenditures equal revenues in a fiscal year.*
3. Budget deficit
   - ▸ *When expenditures exceed revenues in a fiscal year.*
   - ▸ *The 2009 federal budget deficit reached a record $1.42 trillion, or more than $4,700 for every man, woman, and child in the United States.*
   - ▸ *The total federal debt now exceeds $12 trillion.*

B. POLICY TOOLS FOR INFLUENCING THE ECONOMY

1. Monetary policy
   - ▸ *Monetary policy is controlled by the Federal Reserve Board.*
   - ▸ *Monetary policy includes regulating the money supply, controlling inflation, and adjusting interest rates.*
2. Fiscal policy
   - ▸ *Fiscal policy is controlled by the executive and legislative branches. The president proposes the federal budget and Congress passes it.*
   - ▸ *Fiscal policy includes raising and lowering taxes and government spending programs.*

II. SOURCES OF FEDERAL INCOME

A. INDIVIDUAL INCOME TAX

1. The Sixteenth Amendment (1913) permitted Congress to levy an income tax.
2. Income taxes can be progressive or regressive:
   - *A progressive tax is proportionate to income. As a taxpayer's income increases, so does the tax rate.*
   - *A regressive tax is levied at a flat rate without regard to the level of a taxpayer's income or ability to pay. As a result, poor citizens pay a higher percentage of their income compared with wealthier citizens.*
3. Individual income taxes generate approximately 46 percent of federal tax revenue.

B. CORPORATE TAXES

1. Corporations pay a tax that ranges from 15 percent to 35 percent of taxable income.
2. Corporate income taxes generated approximately 12 percent of federal tax revenue.

C. SOCIAL INSURANCE TAXES

1. Employers and employees each pay a Social Security tax equal to 6.2 percent of the first $106,800 of earnings.
2. For Medicare, employees pay a 1.45 percent tax on their total annual income. Employers must match the amounts withheld from their employees' paychecks.
3. The social insurance taxes are regressive because they are levied at a fixed rate without regard to the level of a taxpayer's income.
4. Social insurance taxes now generate approximately 36 percent of federal tax revenue.

D. EXCISE TAXES

1. An excise tax is a tax on the manufacture, sale, or consumption of a good or service.

2. Federal excise taxes are currently imposed on the sale of gasoline, tobacco, alcohol, airline tickets, and many other goods and services.

3. Excise taxes currently generate approximately 2.7 percent of federal tax revenue.

E. ESTATE AND GIFT TAXES

1. An estate tax is a levy imposed on the assets of someone who dies. A gift tax is a levy imposed on a gift from a living person to another.

2. Estate taxes currently generate 1.2 percent of federal tax revenue.

F. CUSTOM DUTIES

1. Custom duties or tariffs are taxes levied on goods brought into the United States from abroad.

2. Prior to the income tax, custom duties were the federal government's most important source of income. They currently generate just 1.1 percent of federal tax revenue.

 ## III. FEDERAL EXPENDITURES

A. UNCONTROLLABLE SPENDING

1. Congress and the president have no power to directly change uncontrollable spending.

2. Over 60 percent of all federal spending now falls into the uncontrollable category.

3. Entitlement programs
   ▸ *A federal entitlement is a program that guarantees a specific level of benefits to persons who meet requirements set by law.*
   ▸ *Social Security, Medicare, Medicaid, food stamps, unemployment insurance, and veterans' pensions and benefits are the largest entitlement programs.*
   ▸ *Entitlement programs are by far the largest portion of uncontrollable spending in the federal budget. Social*

Security, Medicare, and Medicaid are now responsible for approximately 44 percent of all federal expenditures.

Be sure you understand that entitlement programs represent the largest portion of uncontrollable spending in the federal budget. Entitlements thus represent a formidable barrier to achieving a balanced budget.

4. Borrowing
  ▸ *The federal debt now exceeds $12 trillion.*
  ▸ *Approximately 5 to 9 percent of all federal expenditures go to paying interest on the debt. It is important to note that the amount of money spent servicing the debt depends on interest rates. If interest rates rise, then the amount required to service the debt will also rise.*

B. DISCRETIONARY SPENDING

1. Discretionary spending programs are not required by law.
2. Defense, education, agriculture, highways, research grants, and government operations are all examples of discretionary programs.
3. Defense currently accounts for approximately 20 percent of the total federal budget.

IV. THE BUDGETARY PROCESS

A. THE PRESIDENT AND THE BUDGET

1. The president initiates the budget process by submitting a proposed budget to Congress.
2. The Office of Management and Budget (OMB) has the primary responsibility for preparing the federal budget.
3. The budget reflects the priorities and goals of the president's policy agenda.

B. CONGRESS AND THE BUDGET

1. The Congressional Budget and Impoundment Control Act of 1974
   - ▸ *Designed to reform the congressional budgetary process and regain power previously lost to the executive branch.*
   - ▸ *Created a fixed budget calendar.*
   - ▸ *Established a budget committee in each house of Congress.*
   - ▸ *Created the Congressional Budget Office (CBO) to advise Congress by forecasting revenues and evaluating the probable consequences of budget decisions.*
2. The president's budget is sent to both the House and Senate Appropriations Committees, which hold hearings on key items.
3. All tax proposals are referred to the House Ways and Means Committee and to the Senate Finance Committee.
4. Congress is required to pass thirteen major appropriations bills by the beginning of the federal government's fiscal year on October 1.

C. BUDGET BARRIERS TO ACHIEVING A BALANCED BUDGET

1. Entitlement programs now account for over 60 percent of the total federal budget. This limits what the president and Congress can do to achieve a balanced budget.
2. Federal agencies assume that their annual budgets will increase by a small amount each year. This process of small but regular increases is called incrementalism. Because it is built into the budgetary process, it is very difficult to make spending cuts.
3. The fragmented federal system enables interest groups to successfully resist tax increases and defend favored programs.

D. CONSEQUENCES OF BUDGET DEFICITS

1. Budget deficits require huge interest payments. In 2008, the federal government paid $249 billion just to service the debt.
2. Budget deficits will place a heavy burden on future generations.
3. Budget deficits make it difficult to fully fund key policy goals.

KEY CONTENT REVIEW

V. SOCIAL SECURITY

A. BACKGROUND

1. Franklin D. Roosevelt signed the Social Security Act into law in 1935.

2. In 1965, Congress added Medicare to the Social Security program. Medicare is designed to assist the elderly with medical costs.

3. Social Security and Medicare are the most expensive programs in the federal budget. Along with Medicaid, they currently comprise approximately 44 percent of all federal expenditures.

B. DEMOGRAPHIC TRENDS THAT THREATEN THE FUTURE OF THE SOCIAL SECURITY PROGRAM

1. When the Social Security program began, there were 25 workers for every 1 beneficiary. Today the ratio is 3.3 workers for every 1 beneficiary.

2. The Baby Boom generation includes 76 million people born between 1946 and 1964. As the Baby Boom generation begins to retire, the number of workers who fund Social Security will decline while the number of people eligible for Social Security benefits will increase.

3. As a result of improved health care, average life expectancy is increasing. This will put additional pressure on the Social Security system.

AP U.S. Government and Politics exams have thus far not devoted any multiple-choice or free-response questions to foreign policy and national security. In contrast, they have devoted a number of questions to Social Security. It is very important for you to study the demographic forces that are combining to threaten the solvency of the Social Security system.

Civil Liberties

 I. **INTRODUCTION**

A. KEY TERMS

1. Civil liberties
   - ▸ *Civil liberties are legal and constitutional rights that protect individuals from arbitrary acts of government.*
   - ▸ *Civil liberties include freedom of speech, freedom of religion, and freedom of the press, as well as guarantees of a fair trial.*
2. Civil rights
   - ▸ *Civil rights are policies designed to protect people against arbitrary or discriminatory treatment by government officials or individuals.*
   - ▸ *Civil rights include laws against racial and gender discrimination.*

B. THE BILL OF RIGHTS

1. The Constitution, as originally written, contained a number of specific rights and restrictions on government authority. For example, the new government could not grant titles of nobility or require a religious oath for holding a federal office.
2. When Anti-Federalists objected to the absence of a bill of rights, the Federalists pledged that the First Congress would draw up a list of safeguards to protect basic rights and freedoms.
3. Led by James Madison, the First Congress passed ten amendments popularly known as the Bill of Rights. When the states ratified these amendments in 1791, they became part of the Constitution.

II. **THE BILL OF RIGHTS AND THE STATES**

A. THE SCOPE OF THE BILL OF RIGHTS

1. In 1791, every state constitution included a bill of rights. The first ten amendments were intended to restrict the new federal government, not the existing state governments. It is important to note that the First Amendment begins with the words, "Congress shall make no law . . . "

2. *Barron v. Baltimore* (1833)
   ▸ *John Barron co-owned a profitable wharf in Baltimore Harbor. He complained that the city of Baltimore damaged his business when a construction project made the water too shallow for most vessels. Barron argued that the Fifth Amendment required the city of Baltimore to provide him with just compensation.*
   ▸ *Led by Chief Justice John Marshall, the Supreme Court unanimously ruled that the Bill of Rights "contains no expression indicating an intention to apply them to the state governments. This court cannot so apply them."*
   ▸ *The Supreme Court thus established a precedent that the freedoms guaranteed by the Bill of Rights did not restrict the state governments.*

B. THE FOURTEENTH AMENDMENT

1. Ratified in 1868, the Fourteenth Amendment declared, "No state shall make or enforce any law which shall abridge the privileges or immunities of citizens of the United States nor shall any state deprive any person of life, liberty, or property, without due process of law; nor deny to any person within its jurisdiction the equal protection of the laws."

2. The Fourteenth Amendment contains two key clauses that have had a significant impact on Supreme Court decisions and U.S. politics:
   ▸ *The Due Process Clause*
   ▸ *The Equal Protection Clause*

C. *GITLOW V. NEW YORK* (1925)

1. Benjamin Gitlow wrote a pamphlet entitled "The Revolutionary Age" urging industrial workers to strike and join in a revolution to overthrow organized government.

2. Gitlow was arrested and convicted for violating a New York state law that made it a crime to advocate the overthrow of the government by force or violence.

3. Gitlow argued that the New York law violated his right to freedom of speech and the press.

4. The Supreme Court voted to uphold Gitlow's conviction. However, the Court also ruled that "freedom of speech and of the press . . . are among the fundamental and personal rights and liberties protected by the Due Process Clause of the Fourteenth Amendment from impairment by the states . . . "

D. THE INCORPORATION DOCTRINE

1. In *Barron v. Baltimore*, the Supreme Court ruled that the federal courts could not stop the enforcement of state laws that restricted the rights enumerated in the Bill of Rights.

2. The Supreme Court's decision in *Gitlow v. New York* began the incorporation process of using the Due Process Clause of the Fourteenth Amendment to extend most of the requirements of the Bill of Rights to the states.

3. The incorporation process did not occur at once. Instead, it has been a gradual process by which the Supreme Court has used a series of individual decisions to incorporate the Bill of Rights into the Due Process Clause of the Fourteenth Amendment.

The process of selective incorporation generated several multiple-choice questions and a free-response question on the 2005 exam. It is very important to know how the Supreme Court has used the Due Process Clause of the Fourteenth Amendment to apply protections in the Bill of Rights to the states. Be sure that you can discuss how the rights of criminal defendants and privacy rights have been incorporated.

III. FREEDOM OF RELIGION

A. THE FIRST AMENDMENT

1. America's religious liberties originated in colonial opposition to government-sponsored churches.

2. The First Amendment contains two fundamental guarantees of religious freedom:
   ▸ *The Establishment Clause prohibiting "an establishment of religion . . . "*
   ▸ *The Free Exercise Clause prohibiting government from interfering with the practice of religion.*
3. It is important to note that both of these protections have been extended to the states by the Due Process Clause of the Fourteenth Amendment.

B. THE ESTABLISHMENT CLAUSE

1. "A wall of separation between Church and State"
   ▸ *Thomas Jefferson contended that the First Amendment created a "wall of separation between Church and State," forbidding any government support for religion.*
   ▸ *Although Americans have traditionally opposed the creation of a national church, school prayer and aid to church-related schools have sparked controversial court cases that resulted in landmark Supreme Court decisions.*
2. School prayer: *Engel v. Vitale* (1962)
   ▸ *In 1951, the New York State Board of Regents approved the following prayer for recital each morning in New York public schools: "Almighty God, we acknowledge our dependence upon Thee, and we beg Thy blessings upon us, our parents, our teachers, and our country."*
   ▸ *Steven Engel, the father of two children in the New Hyde Park public schools, objected when the local school board adopted the prayer and directed it be said aloud at the beginning of each school day.*
   ▸ *Engel argued that the Regents' prayer violated the Establishment Clause of the First Amendment as applied to the states through the Fourteenth Amendment.*
   ▸ *The Supreme Court ruled that state-sponsored prayer in public schools was an unconstitutional violation of the Establishment Clause that "breaks the constitutional wall of separation between Church and State."*
3. Aid to parochial schools: *Lemon v. Kurtzman* (1971)
   ▸ *Pennsylvania's 1968 Nonpublic Elementary and Secondary Education Act allowed the state Superintendent of Public Instruction to reimburse church-related schools for secular textbooks, secular*

instructional materials, and the salaries of teachers who taught secular subjects.

▸ *The Supreme Court declared that aid to church-related schools must meet the following three tests: First, a government's action must have a secular legislative purpose. Second, the government's action must neither advance nor inhibit religion. And third, the government's action must not foster an "excessive entanglement" between government and religion.*

▸ *Based on the "Lemon test," the Supreme Court struck down the Pennsylvania law, saying that state funding for private religious schools violates the Establishment Clause of the First Amendment.*

C. THE FREE EXERCISE CLAUSE

1. General points

   ▸ *The First Amendment's Free Exercise Clause guarantees each person the right to believe what they want.*

   ▸ *However, a religion cannot make an act legal that would otherwise be illegal. The government can act when religious practices violate criminal laws, offend public morals, or threaten community safety. For example, in* Oregon v. Smith *(1990), the Supreme Court banned the use of illegal drugs in religious ceremonies.*

2. Limits on the Free Exercise Clause: *Reynolds v. United States* (1879)

   ▸ *George Reynolds was a member of the Mormon Church who married two women. Reynolds argued that his conviction for polygamy should be overturned because it was his religious duty to marry multiple times.*

   ▸ *The Supreme Court made an important distinction between religious beliefs and religious practices. The Court cannot restrict what a person believes because that "lies solely between a man and his God." However, society has a right to legislate against religious activities that violate a law of the land.*

   ▸ *The Supreme Court ruled against Reynolds, arguing that permitting polygamy would "make the professed doctrines of religious belief superior to the law of the land, and in effect to permit every citizen to become a law unto himself."*

IV. FREEDOM OF SPEECH AND PRESS

A. THE DEFENSE OF FREE SPEECH

1. The First Amendment
   ▸ *The Framers believed that the right to free speech is a fundamental natural right. The First Amendment clearly states that, "Congress shall make no law . . . abridging the freedom of speech or of the press."*
   ▸ *The First and Fourteenth Amendments protect free speech from incursions of both the federal and state governments.*

2. Protections of unpopular views
   ▸ *The guarantees of free speech are intended to protect the expressions of unpopular views. "The freedom to differ," Justice Jackson wrote, "is not limited to things that do not matter much."*
   ▸ *Even if a doctrine is "wrong," it does not follow that it should be silenced. The English philosopher John Stuart Mill argued that wrong or offensive ideas force us to sharpen our own views. If we believe in free expression, we must believe in its power to overcome error in a fair debate.*

B. THE "CLEAR AND PRESENT DANGER" TEST

1. The Espionage Act of 1917 prohibited forms of dissent deemed to be harmful to the nation's war effort in World War I.

2. Charles Schenck, the general secretary of the American Socialist Party, strongly opposed America's participation in World War I. He mailed 15,000 leaflets to potential draftees comparing military conscription to slavery. Schenck urged his readers to "assert your rights" by resisting the military draft.

3. The government responded by arresting Schenck for violating the Espionage Act. Schenck argued that the Espionage Act was unconstitutional because it violated the First Amendment's promises of free speech.

4. Speaking for the majority, Justice Oliver Wendell Holmes wrote, "[T]he character of every act depends on the circumstances in which it is done. The most stringent protection of free speech would not protect a man in falsely

shouting fire in a theatre, and causing a panic. . . . The question in every case is whether the words used are used in such circumstances and are of such a nature as to create a clear and present danger that they will bring about the substantive evils that Congress has the right to prevent."

5. The clear and present danger test created a precedent that First Amendment guarantees of free speech are not absolute.

6. In *Brandenburg v. Ohio* (1969), the Supreme Court limited the clear and present danger test by ruling that the government could punish the advocacy of illegal action only if "such advocacy is directed to inciting or producing imminent lawless action and is likely to incite or produce such action."

C. LIMITS ON FREE SPEECH

1. Libel and slander
   - *Libel is a written defamation that falsely attacks a person's good name and reputation.*
   - *Slander is a spoken defamation that falsely attacks a person's good name and reputation.*
   - *In the* New York Times v. Sullivan *(1964), the Supreme Court ruled that statements about public figures are libelous only when they are both false and purposely malicious.*

2. Obscenity
   - *In* Roth v. United States *(1957), the Supreme Court ruled that "[o]bscenity is not within the area of constitutionally protected speech or press."*
   - *In* Miller v. California *(1973), the Court listed a number of tests for obscenity. It is important to note that it is up to each community to implement these tests.*

3. Symbolic speech
   - *Symbolic speech includes forms of nonverbal communication such as carrying signs, wearing armbands, and burning flags.*
   - *In 1965, high school students John and Mary Beth Tinker protested the Vietnam War by wearing black armbands containing a peace symbol. When the Tinkers refused to remove their armbands, they were sent home for violating a school board policy banning armbands. In* Tinker v. Des Moines Independent School District

(1969), the Supreme Court ruled that the school board's action violated the First and Fourteenth Amendment's protection of free expression. Writing for the majority, Justice Abe Fortas stated that students and teachers do not "shed their constitutional rights to freedom of speech or expression at the school house gate."

▸ *In 1984, Gregory Johnson burned an American flag during a rally outside the Republican National Convention in Dallas, Texas. Texas state authorities prosecuted Johnson for violating a state law forbidding the "desecration of a venerated object." In* Texas v. Johnson *(1989), the Supreme Court ruled that flag burning is a form of symbolic speech protected by the First Amendment.*

▸ *It is important to note that the Supreme Court has ruled that the First Amendment does not protect symbolic speech intended to incite illegal actions. For example, states may make it a crime to burn a cross with the intent to threaten racial terror.*

D. PRIOR RESTRAINT

1. Prior restraint is the attempt to limit freedom of press by preventing material from being published. Prior restraint is thus a form of censorship.

2. The Supreme Court has repeatedly ruled that prior restraint is a violation of the First Amendment protection of freedom of press. Important test cases have included *Near v. Minnesota* (1931) and *New York Times Company v. United States* (1971).

3. It is important to note that public school officials do have a broad power to censor school newspapers. In *Hazelwood School District v. Kuhlmeier* (1988), the Supreme Court ruled that school administrators can exercise "editorial control over the style and content of student speech in school-sponsored expressive activities so long as their actions are reasonably related to legitimate pedagogical concerns."

V. RIGHTS OF THE ACCUSED

A. RIGHTS IN THE ORIGINAL CONSTITUTION

1. A writ of habeas corpus
   - ▸ *The Constitution expressly states, "The Privilege of the Writ of Habeas Corpus shall not be suspended, unless when in Cases of Rebellion or Invasion the public safety may require it."*
   - ▸ *A writ of habeas corpus is a court order directing that a prisoner be brought before a court and that court officers show cause why the prisoner should not be released. The writ of habeas corpus thus prevents unjust arrests and imprisonments.*

2. Bills of attainder
   - ▸ *The Constitution prohibits Congress and the state legislatures from passing a bill of attainder.*
   - ▸ *A bill of attainder is a legislative act that provides for the the punishment of a person without a court trial.*

3. Ex post facto laws
   - ▸ *The Constitution expressly prohibits Congress and the state legislatures from enacting ex post facto laws.*
   - ▸ *An ex post facto law is a law applied to an act committed before the law was enacted.*

B. SEARCHES AND SEIZURES

1. The Fourth Amendment declares, "The right of the people to be secure in their persons, houses, papers, and effects, against unreasonable searches and seizures, shall not be violated . . . ."

2. The exclusionary rule
   - ▸ *The exclusionary rule prohibits evidence obtained by illegal searches or seizures from being admitted in court.*
   - ▸ *The Supreme Court first established the exclusionary rule in* Weeks v. United States *(1914). Although Weeks was a landmark decision case, the Court's decision applied only to federal cases.*
   - ▸ *The Supreme Court extended the exclusionary rule to the states in* Mapp v. Ohio *(1961). This case illustrates the process of incorporation by which the Fourth*

Amendment was applied to the states through the Due
Process Clause of the Fourteenth Amendment.

C. THE RIGHT TO COUNSEL

1. The Sixth Amendment states, "The accused shall enjoy the
   right . . . to have the assistance of counsel for his defense."
   It is important to note that when the Sixth Amendment was
   ratified, this right did not apply to people tried in state courts.

2. *Gideon v. Wainwright* (1963)

   ▸ *Clarence Earl Gideon was accused of breaking and
     entering a Florida poolroom and stealing a small amount
     of money.*

   ▸ *The judge refused Gideon's request for a court-appointed
     free lawyer.*

   ▸ *Gideon appealed his conviction, arguing that by refusing
     to appoint a lawyer to help him, the Florida court
     violated rights promised by the Sixth and Fourteenth
     Amendments.*

   ▸ *In a unanimous decision, the Supreme Court ruled that
     the Sixth Amendment right-to-counsel provision applies
     to those accused of major crimes under state laws. This
     landmark case illustrates the process of incorporation,
     by which the Sixth Amendment was applied to the
     states through the Due Process Clause of the Fourteenth
     Amendment.*

D. THE MIRANDA RULE

1. The Fifth Amendment forbids forced self-incrimination,
   stating that no person "shall be compelled to be a witness
   against himself."

2. *Miranda v. Arizona* (1966)

   ▸ *Ernesto Miranda was a mentally challenged drifter
     accused of kidnapping and raping an 18-year-old
     woman near Phoenix.*

   ▸ *After two hours of police interrogation, Miranda signed
     a written confession. The police did not inform Miranda
     of his constitutional rights at any time during the
     questioning.*

   ▸ *The Supreme Court overturned Miranda's conviction,
     declaring that the police must inform criminal suspects*

of their constitutional rights before questioning suspects after arrest.

▸ *The Miranda rules include informing a suspect that he or she has the right to remain silent, to stop answering questions at any time, and the right to have a lawyer present during questioning. Suspects must also be told that what they say can be used against them in a court of law.*

 # THE RIGHT TO PRIVACY AND ABORTION RIGHTS

A. THE RIGHT TO PRIVACY

1. Justice Louis D. Brandeis defined privacy as "the right to be left alone."

2. The Bill of Rights does not specifically grant Americans a right to privacy. However, the following constitutional provisions imply a right to privacy:
   ▸ *The First Amendment's guarantee of freedom of religion.*
   ▸ *The Third Amendment's prohibition against the government forcing citizens to quarter soldiers in their homes.*
   ▸ *The Fourth Amendment's protection against unreasonable searches and seizures.*
   ▸ *The Fifth Amendment's rule that private property cannot be seized without "due process of law."*

B. *GRISWOLD V. CONNECTICUT* (1965)

1. Estelle Griswold, the executive director of the Planned Parenthood League of Connecticut, challenged the constitutionality of an 1879 Connecticut law that prohibited the use of "any drug, medicinal article or instrument for the purpose of preventing conception."

2. The Supreme Court ruled that the Connecticut law criminalizing the use of contraceptives violated the right to marital privacy.

3. Writing for the majority, Justice William O. Douglas argued that the right to privacy was found in the unstated liberties implied by the explicitly stated rights in the Bill of Rights.

4. The right to privacy established in *Griswold v. Connecticut* set an important precedent for *Roe v. Wade.*

C. *ROE V. WADE* (1973)

1. Jane Roe (a pseudonym for Norma McCorvey) challenged the constitutionality of a Texas law allowing abortions only to save the life of the mother.
2. Roe argued that the decision to obtain an abortion should be protected by the right to privacy implied by the Bill of Rights.
3. The Supreme Court struck down the Texas law by a vote of 7 to 2.

D. CHALLENGES TO ROE

1. In *Webster v. Reproductive Health Services* (1989), the Supreme Court upheld a Missouri law prohibiting abortions (except those preserving the mother's life) in any publicly operated hospital or clinic in Missouri.
2. In *Planned Parenthood of Southeastern Pennsylvania v. Casey* (1992), the Supreme Court ruled that a state may place reasonable limits that do not place an "undue burden" on a woman's right to have an abortion. For example, a state may impose a 24-hour waiting period and require parental consent for minors.

Test Tip

Each AP U.S. Government and Politics exam contains questions devoted to Supreme Court cases. **Miranda v. Arizona** *and* **Roe v. Wade** *have generated the most multiple-choice questions. It is important to remember that the "Miranda warning" protects criminal suspects against unfair police interrogation. It is also important to remember that the* **Roe v. Wade** *decision was based on the right to privacy established in* **Griswold v. Connecticut.**

Civil Rights

I. CONCEPTIONS OF EQUALITY

A. THE DECLARATION OF INDEPENDENCE

1. Thomas Jefferson famously declared that "all men are created equal."
2. U.S. political culture has interpreted Jefferson's assertion to mean a belief in political equality, legal equality, and equality of opportunity.
3. U.S. political culture does not support economic equality.

B. THE CONSTITUTION

1. Neither the Constitution nor the Bill of Rights uses the word *equality*.
2. The Fourteenth Amendment
   ▸ *The Fourteenth Amendment forbids the states from denying any person "the equal protection of the laws."*
   ▸ *The Equal Protection Clause has played a key role in the struggle to provide civil rights to all Americans.*

C. THE SUPREME COURT

1. Reasonable classification
   ▸ *The Supreme Court has ruled that government must have the power to make reasonable classifications between persons and groups.*
   ▸ *Reasonable classifications include denying the vote to citizens under the age of 18 or imposing a high excise tax on the sale of cigarettes which smokers must pay.*

2. Strict scrutiny
   ▸ *The Supreme Court has ruled that classification by race and ethnic background is inherently suspect and must therefore meet a strict scrutiny test.*
   ▸ *Classification based on race and ethnic background must be justified by a "compelling public interest."*

II. THE STRUGGLE FOR RACIAL EQUALITY

A. THE *DRED SCOTT* DECISION, 1857

1. In *Dred Scott v. Sandford* (1857), the Supreme Court ruled that Black people were not citizens of the United States and therefore could not petition the Court.
2. The *Dred Scott* decision established the principle that national legislation could not limit the spread of slavery into the territories.
3. The *Dred Scott* decision repealed the Northwest Ordinance of 1787 and the Missouri Compromise of 1820.

B. THE RECONSTRUCTION AMENDMENTS

1. The Thirteenth Amendment abolished slavery and involuntary servitude.
2. The Fourteenth Amendment made former slaves citizens, thus invalidating the *Dred Scott* decision. The amendment's Due Process and Equal Protection clauses were designed to protect the rights of newly freed African American citizens against infringement by state governments.
3. The Fifteenth Amendment provided suffrage for African American males.

C. *PLESSY V. FERGUSON* (1896)

1. The case involved a dispute over the legality of a Louisiana law requiring "equal but separate accommodations for the white and colored races" on railroad coaches.
2. The Supreme Court upheld the law, ruling that segregated public facilities were constitutional so long as the accommodations were "separate but equal."

3. The Court's "separate but equal" doctrine sanctioned segregation and strengthened the states at the expense of the federal government.

D. *BROWN V. BOARD OF EDUCATION OF TOPEKA* (1954)

1. Led by Chief Justice Earl Warren, the Supreme Court ruled that racially segregated schools violated the Equal Protection Clause of the Fourteenth Amendment.
2. The Supreme Court reversed the principle of "separate but equal" by declaring that racially segregated schools are inherently unequal.

E. THE CIVIL RIGHTS ACT OF 1964

1. The bill finally passed when the Senate invoked cloture to end a filibuster that lasted 83 days.
2. The act did the following:
   ‣ *Ended Jim Crow segregation by making racial discrimination illegal in hotels, motels, restaurants, and other places of public accommodation.*
   ‣ *Prohibited discrimination in employment on the basis of race, color, national origin, religion, or gender.*
   ‣ *Created the Equal Employment Opportunity Commission to monitor and enforce protections against job discrimination.*
   ‣ *Authorized the Department of Justice to initiate lawsuits to desegregate public facilities and schools.*
   ‣ *Prohibited discrimination in employment on grounds of race, color, religion, national origin, or sex.*
3. The Supreme Court upheld the provisions outlawing segregation in places of public accommodation by ruling that such segregation involved interstate commerce and thus fell under the legislative authority of Congress.

Test Tip

AP U.S. Government and Politics test writers have devoted a significant number of multiple-choice questions to **Brown v. Board of Education of Topeka** *and the Civil Rights Act of 1964. Be sure that you know that* **Brown** *used the Equal Protection Clause of the Fourteenth Amendment to reverse* **Plessy v. Ferguson.** *Also be sure you know that the Court used the interstate commerce provision of the Constitution to uphold the legality of the Civil Rights Act of 1964.*

III. THE STRUGGLE FOR AFRICAN AMERICAN VOTING RIGHTS

A. METHODS OF DISENFRANCHISING AFRICAN AMERICAN VOTERS

1. Poll taxes required voters to pay a special tax in order to vote.
2. Literacy or "understanding" tests required voters to pass difficult reading comprehension questions before they could register to vote.
3. White primaries excluded African Americans from voting in primary elections.
4. By 1960, only 29 percent of African Americans of voting age were registered to vote in the South. In contrast, 61 percent of whites were registered.

B. ELIMINATING THE POLL TAX

1. The Twenty-Fourth Amendment (1964) prohibited poll taxes in federal elections.
2. In 1966, the Supreme Court voided poll taxes in state elections.

C. THE VOTING RIGHTS ACT OF 1965

1. Outlawed literacy tests and other discriminatory practices that had been responsible for disenfranchising African American voters.
2. Provided for federal oversight of voter registration in areas with a history of discriminatory voting practices.
3. Significantly improved the voter registration disparity between whites and African Americans. As the number of African American voters increased, so did the number of African American elected officials. In 1965, only about 70 African Americans held public office in the 11 Southern states. By the early twenty-first century the number soared to over 5,000.

D. RACIAL GERRYMANDERING

1. Following the 1990 census, several state legislatures created oddly shaped districts designed to give minority group voters a numerical majority.

2. In *Shaw v. Reno* (1993), the Supreme Court ruled that oddly shaped minority-majority districts would be held to a standard of strict scrutiny under the Equal Protection Clause.

3. Subsequent Supreme Court decisions refined the *Shaw* ruling by holding that the use of race as a "predominant factor" in drawing district lines should be presumed to be unconstitutional.

IV. WOMEN'S STRUGGLE FOR CIVIL RIGHTS

A. ORIGINAL STATUS OF WOMEN

1. Although women were considered citizens, they had no political rights.

2. Women were subjected to a male-dominated system of family law. For example, women could not divorce their husbands, sign contracts, or dispose of property.

3. Women were denied educational and career opportunities. For example, in 1873, the Supreme Court denied the right of women to practice law, saying, "The paramount destiny and mission of women are to fulfill the noble and benign offices of wife and mother. This is the law of the Creator."

B. THE SENECA FALLS CONVENTION, 1848

1. Elizabeth Cady Stanton and Lucretia Mott organized and led the Seneca Falls Convention.

2. The convention adopted resolutions calling for the abolition of legal, economic, and social discrimination against women.

C. THE FIGHT FOR SUFFRAGE

1. Women's rights activists were bitterly disappointed when the Fifteenth Amendment failed to grant women the right to vote.

2. The Nineteenth Amendment (1920) guaranteed women the right to vote.

D. THE EQUAL RIGHTS AMENDMENT

1. Congress passed the Equal Rights Amendment (ERA) in 1972. The amendment provided that "[e]quality of rights under the

law shall not be denied or abridged by the United States or by any state on account of sex."

2. The ERA fell three states short of the three-fourths necessary for ratification.

E. MILESTONES IN THE MODERN WOMEN'S RIGHTS MOVEMENT

1. The Equal Pay Act of 1963 requires employers to pay women and men equal pay for equal work. Nonetheless, women still earn only $0.81 for every $1.00 men make.

2. The Civil Rights Act of 1964 prohibited discrimination in employment based on race and sex.

3. In 1966, Betty Friedan and other leading feminists founded the National Organization of Women to challenge sex discrimination in the workplace.

4. *Reed v. Reed* (1971)
   ▸ *The Supreme Court ruled that an Idaho law that automatically preferred a father over a mother as executor of a son's estate violated the Equal Protection Clause of the Fourteenth Amendment.*
   ▸ *The* Reed *decision created a new standard for judging constitutionality in sex discrimination cases. The Supreme Court ruled that any law that classifies people on the basis of gender "must be reasonable, not arbitrary, and must rest on some ground of difference." That difference must serve "important government objectives" and must be substantially related to those objectives.*

5. Title IX of the Education Act of 1972 forbids educational institutions receiving federal funds from discriminating against female students. This provision has played a pivotal role in the development of women's athletic programs.

V. AFFIRMATIVE ACTION

A. BACKGROUND

1. In 1965, President Johnson issued an executive order requiring all contractors and unions doing business with

the federal government to take affirmative action in hiring minorities. Two years later, this order was amended to extend affirmative action to women.

2. Affirmative action is a policy requiring federal agencies, universities, and most employers to take positive steps to remedy the effects of past discrimination.

B. THE DEBATE OVER AFFIRMATIVE ACTION

1. Supporters
   ▸ *Supporters believe that affirmative action is needed to make up for past injustices. "Freedom is not enough," insisted President Johnson. "You do not take a person who for years has been hobbled by chains and liberate him, bring him to the starting line of a race and then say, 'you are free to compete with all the others' and still justly believe that you have been completely fair."*
   ▸ *Supporters also argue that increasing the number of women and minorities in desirable jobs is an important social goal.*

2. Critics
   ▸ *Critics argue that affirmative action programs create reverse discrimination that unfairly penalizes members of the majority group.*
   ▸ *Critics also contend that laws and policies should promote equal opportunity, not equal results.*

C. *REGENTS OF THE UNIVERSITY OF CALIFORNIA V. BAKKE* (1978)

1. The Medical School of the University of California at Davis opened in 1968 with an entering class of 50 students. The new school did not have an admissions program for disadvantaged or minority students. The first class included no African American, Mexican American, or American Indian students.

2. In 1971, the medical school increased the size of its entering class to 100 students. To address the absence of minority students, the Regents created a special plan in which 16 of the 100 spaces in each entering class were set aside for "disadvantaged" or "minority" applicants. Candidates for the 16 special slots did not have to meet the same academic standards as the other applicants.

3. Allan Bakke, a 37-year-old white NASA engineer, applied for admission to the Medical School at the University of California at Davis. The medical school rejected Bakke's application, even though his test scores were higher than those of all the minority candidates who were accepted.

4. Supreme Court decisions:

   ▸ *The Supreme Court ruled that the medical school's strict quota system denied Bakke the equal protection guaranteed by the Fourteenth Amendment. The Court therefore ordered the medical school to admit Bakke as a student.*

   ▸ *At the same time, the Court also ruled that both the Constitution and the 1964 Civil Rights Act do allow race to be used as one factor among others in the competition for available places.*

D. RECENT AFFIRMATIVE ACTION CASES

1. In *Grutter v. Bollinger* (2003), the Supreme Court upheld the affirmative action policy of the University of Michigan Law School. The decision upheld the *Bakke* ruling that race could be a consideration on admissions policy, but that quotas are illegal.

2. In *Gratz v. Bollinger* (2003), the Supreme Court struck down a University of Michigan undergraduate admissions policy that automatically awarded applicants from underrepresented racial and minority groups 20 of the 100 points needed to guarantee admission. The Court ruled that this point system violated the Equal Protection Clause of the Fourteenth Amendment because it was tantamount to creating a quota system.

Test Tip

Affirmative action is a controversial issue that has generated heated public debate and a number of test questions. The Supreme Court has consistently ruled against quota systems while affirming the right of organizations to use race as one factor among others in admissions and hiring policies.

PART III:

KEY THEMES AND FACTS

The Top 30 Supreme Court Cases

AP U.S. Government and Politics texts discuss a large number of Supreme Court cases. Is it necessary to make a list of the cases and memorize them? Fortunately, there is a better way of using your valuable study time. This chapter discusses the key decisions in 30 Supreme Court cases that have played a role in multiple-choice and free-response questions. As you study these cases pay attention to their precedents, rules, and standards. Also note how many cases involve the First and Fourteenth Amendments.

I. CLASSIC MARSHALL COURT CASES

1. *Marbury v. Madison* (1803)
    ▸ *Established the principle of judicial review.*
    ▸ *Strengthened the power of the judicial branch by giving the Supreme Court the authority to declare acts of Congress unconstitutional.*
2. *McCulloch v. Maryland* (1819)
    ▸ *Confirmed the right of Congress to utilize implied powers to carry out its expressed powers.*
    ▸ *Validated the supremacy of the national government over the states by declaring that states cannot interfere with or tax the legitimate activities of the federal government.*
3. *Gibbons v. Ogden* (1824)
    ▸ *Strengthened the power of the federal government to regulate interstate commerce.*
    ▸ *Established the commerce clause's role as a key vehicle for the expansion of federal power.*

II. FIRST AMENDMENT: ESTABLISHMENT CLAUSE CASES

4. *Engel v. Vitale* (1962)
    ▸ *Struck down state-sponsored prayer in public schools.*
    ▸ *Ruled that the Regents' prayer was an unconstitutional violation of the Establishment Clause.*

5. *Lemon v. Kurtzman* (1971)
    ▸ *Struck down state funding for private religious schools.*
    ▸ *Ruled that state aid to church-related schools must meet three tests: (a) the purpose of the aid must be clearly secular, (b) the government's action must neither advance nor inhibit religion, and (c) the government's action must not foster an "excessive entanglement" between government and religion.*

III. FIRST AMENDMENT: FREE EXERCISE CLAUSE CASES

6. *Reynolds v. United States* (1879)
    ▸ *Banned polygamy.*
    ▸ *Distinguished between religious beliefs that are protected by the Free Exercise Clause and religious practices that may be restricted.*
    ▸ *Ruled that religious practices cannot make an act legal that would otherwise be illegal.*

7. *Oregon v. Smith* (1990)
    ▸ *Banned the use of illegal drugs in religious ceremonies.*
    ▸ *Ruled that the government can act when religious practices violate criminal laws.*

IV. FIRST AMENDMENT: FREE SPEECH CASES

8. *Schenck v. United States* (1919)
    ▸ *Ruled that free speech could be limited when it presents a "clear and present danger . . . ."*
    ▸ *Established the "clear and present danger" test to define conditions under which public authorities can limit free speech.*

9. *New York Times v. Sullivan* (1964)
    ▸ *Ruled that public officials cannot win a suit for defamation unless the statement is made with "actual malice."*

> ▸ Established the "actual malice" standard to promote "uninhibited, robust, and wide-open" public debate.

10. *Roth v. United States* (1951)
    > ▸ Ruled that obscenity is not constitutionally protected free speech.
    > ▸ Created the "prevailing community standards" rule requiring a consideration of the work as a whole.

11. *Tinker v. Des Moines Independent School District* (1969)
    > ▸ Protected some forms of symbolic speech.
    > ▸ Ruled that students do not "shed their constitutional rights to freedom of speech or expression at the schoolhouse gate."

12. *Texas v. Johnson* (1989)
    > ▸ Ruled that flag burning is a form of symbolic speech protected by the First Amendment.

V. THE FOURTEENTH AMENDMENT: SELECTIVE INCORPORATION CASES

13. *Barron v. Baltimore* (1833)
    > ▸ Ruled that the Bill of Rights cannot be applied to the states.

14. *Gitlow v. New York* (1925)
    > ▸ Established precedent for the doctrine of selective incorporation, thus extending most of the requirements of the Bill of Rights to the states.

VI. THE FOURTEENTH AMENDMENT: DUE PROCESS CLAUSE CASES

15. *Weeks v. United States* (1914)
    > ▸ Established the exclusionary rule in federal cases.
    > ▸ Prohibited evidence obtained by illegal searches and seizures from being admitted in court.

16. *Mapp v. Ohio* (1961)
    > ▸ Extended the exclusionary rule to the states.
    > ▸ Illustrated the process of selective incorporation through the Due Process Clause of the Fourteenth Amendment.

17. *Gideon v. Wainwright* (1963)
   ‣ *Ruled that the Sixth Amendment right-to-counsel provision applies to those accused of major crimes under state laws.*
   ‣ *Illustrated the process of incorporation by which the Sixth Amendment was applied to the states through the Due Process Clause of the Fourteenth Amendment.*

18. *Miranda v. Arizona* (1966)
   ‣ *Ruled that the police must inform criminal suspects of their constitutional rights before questioning suspects after arrest.*
   ‣ *Required police to read the Miranda rules to criminal suspects.*

VII. THE FOURTEENTH AMENDMENT: EQUAL PROTECTION CASES

19. *Dred Scott v. Sandford* (1857)
   ‣ *Ruled that African Americans were not citizens and therefore could not petition the Supreme Court.*
   ‣ *Overturned by the Fourteenth Amendment.*

20. *Plessy v. Ferguson* (1896)
   ‣ *Upheld Jim Crow segregation by approving "separate but equal" public facilities for African Americans.*

21. *Brown v. Board of Education of Topeka* (1954)
   ‣ *Ruled that racially segregated schools violated the Equal Protection Clause of the Fourteenth Amendment.*
   ‣ *Reversed the principle of "separate but equal" established in* Plessy v. Ferguson.

22. *Regents of the University of California v. Bakke* (1978)
   ‣ *Ordered the Medical School at the University of California at Davis to admit Bakke.*
   ‣ *Ruled that the medical school's strict quota system denied Bakke the equal protection guaranteed by the Fourteenth Amendment.*
   ‣ *Ruled that race could be used as one factor among others in the competition for available places.*

23. *Grutter v. Bollinger* (2003)
   ‣ *Upheld the affirmative action policy of the University of Michigan Law School.*

▸ *Upheld the* Bakke *ruling that race could be a consideration in admissions policy but that quotas are illegal.*

VIII. THE RIGHT TO PRIVACY

24. *Griswold v. Connecticut (1965)*
     ▸ *Ruled that a Connecticut law criminalizing the use of contraceptives violated the right to marital privacy.*
     ▸ *Established an important precedent for* Roe v. Wade.

25. *Roe v. Wade (1973)*
     ▸ *Ruled that the decision to obtain an abortion is protected by the right to privacy implied by the Bill of Rights.*

IX. APPORTIONMENT CASES

26. *Baker v. Carr (1962)*
     ▸ *Ruled that the judicial branch of government can rule on matters of legislative apportionment.*
     ▸ *Used the principle of "one person, one vote."*
     ▸ *Ordered state legislative districts to be as equal as possible.*

27. *Wesberry v. Sanders (1963)*
     ▸ *Established the principle of "one person, one vote" in drawing congressional districts.*
     ▸ *Triggered widespread redistricting that gave cities and suburbs greater representation in Congress.*

X. MISCELLANEOUS CASES

28. *Korematsu v. United States (1944)*
     ▸ *Upheld the constitutionality of the relocation of Japanese Americans as a wartime necessity.*
     ▸ *Viewed by contemporary scholars as a flagrant violation of civil liberties.*

29. *United States v. Nixon (1974)*
     ▸ *Ruled that there is no constitutional guarantee of unqualified executive privilege.*

KEY THEMES AND FACTS

30. *Buckley v. Valeo (1976)*
    - ▸ *Upheld federal limits on campaign contributions.*
    - ▸ *Struck down the portion of the Federal Election Campaign Act limiting the amount of money individuals can contribute to their own campaign.*
    - ▸ *Ruled that spending money on one's own campaign is a form of constitutionally protected free speech.*
    - ▸ *Complicated congressional efforts to enact significant campaign finance reform.*

The Top 10 Acts of Congress

AP U.S. Government and Politics texts discuss a large number of congressional acts. Is it necessary to memorize a list of these acts? Fortunately, there is a better way of using your valuable study time. This chapter discusses the key features of 10 congressional acts that have played a role in multiple-choice and free-response questions. As you study each act, pay particular attention to how the act affected the relationship between state governments and the federal government.

1. THE CIVIL RIGHTS ACT OF 1964
   ‣ *Enforced the Fourteenth Amendment.*
   ‣ *Ended Jim Crow segregation in hotels, motels, restaurants, and other places of public accommodation.*
   ‣ *Prohibited discrimination in employment on the basis of race, color, national origin, religion, or gender.*
   ‣ *Created the Equal Employment Opportunity Commission to monitor and enforce protections against job discrimination.*
   ‣ *Prohibited discrimination in employment on grounds of race, color, religion, national origin, or sex.*
   ‣ *Upheld by the Supreme Court on the grounds that segregation affected interstate commerce.*

2. THE VOTING RIGHTS ACT OF 1965
   ‣ *Outlawed literacy tests and other discriminatory practices that had been responsible for disenfranchising African American voters.*
   ‣ *Provided for federal oversight of voter registration in areas with a history of discriminatory voting practices.*
   ‣ *Improved the voter registration disparity between whites and African Americans.*

3. THE CLEAN AIR ACT (1970)
   ▸ *Increased the power of the federal government relative to the power of state governments.*
   ▸ *Established national air quality standards.*
   ▸ *Required states to administer the new standards and to appropriate funds for their implementation.*
   ▸ *Included a provision allowing private citizens to bring lawsuits against individuals and corporations that violated the act.*

4. THE WAR POWERS RESOLUTION (1973)
   ▸ *Enacted to give Congress a greater voice in presidential decisions committing military forces to hostile situations overseas.*
   ▸ *Requires that the president notify Congress within 48 hours of deploying troops.*
   ▸ *Requires the president to bring troops home from hostilities within 60 to 90 days unless Congress extends the time.*

5. THE BUDGET AND IMPOUNDMENT CONTROL ACT OF 1974
   ▸ *Enacted to help Congress regain powers previously lost to the executive branch.*
   ▸ *Created the Congressional Budget Office (CBO) to evaluate the president's budget.*
   ▸ *Established a budget process that includes setting overall levels of revenues and expenditures.*

6. THE FEDERAL ELECTION CAMPAIGN ACT (1974)
   ▸ *Created the Federal Election Commission.*
   ▸ *Tightened reporting requirements for campaign contributions.*
   ▸ *Provided full public financing for major party candidates in the general election.*

7. AMERICANS WITH DISABILITIES ACT (1990)
   ▸ *Increased the power of the federal government relative to the power of the states.*
   ▸ *Requires employers and public facilities to make "reasonable accommodations" for people with disabilities.*
   ▸ *Prohibits discrimination against people with disabilities in employment.*

▸ *Extends the protections of the Civil Rights Act of 1964 to people with physical or mental disabilities.*

8. WELFARE REFORM ACT (1996)

    ▸ *Increased the power of the states relative to the federal government.*

    ▸ *Replaced the Aid to Families with Dependent Children program with block grants to the states.*

    ▸ *Illustrated the process of devolution by giving states greater discretion to determine how to implement the federal goal of transferring people from welfare to work.*

9. NO CHILD LEFT BEHIND ACT (2001)

    ▸ *Requires the states to set standards and measurable goals that can improve individual outcomes in education.*

    ▸ *Requires the states to develop assessments in basic skills to be given to all students in certain grades.*

    ▸ *Represents a dramatic expansion of the federal role in education.*

10. USA PATRIOT ACT (2001)

    ▸ *Expands the definition of terrorism to include domestic terrorism.*

    ▸ *Authorized searches of a home or business without the owner's or the occupant's permission or knowledge.*

    ▸ *Increases the ability of law enforcement agencies to search telephone, e-mail communications, medical, financial, and other records.*

The Top 20 Topics

AP U.S. Government and Politics texts discuss a large number of topics, ranging from the Articles of Confederation to the election of President Obama. This chapter is designed to provide you with a fast review of targeted key topics. Taken together, these 20 topics have generated approximately one-third of all multiple-choice and one-fourth of all free-response questions. A careful review of these topics will help you build a coalition of points that will make an important contribution to your goal of earning a 4 or 5 on the exam.

1. **THE INCUMBENCY ADVANTAGE**
   ▸ *Incumbency is the single most important factor in determining the outcome of congressional elections.*
   ▸ *Incumbent members of the House of Representatives are more likely to be reelected than are incumbent senators.*
   ▸ *Incumbents are able to use "pork barrel politics" to get money for projects that benefit their districts. This helps incumbents earn a reputation for service to their constituents.*
   ▸ *Incumbents can take advantage of the franking privilege, which enables them to send mail to their constituents at the government's expense.*

2. **FEDERALISM**
   ▸ *Federalism is a system of government in which power is divided by a written constitution between a central government and regional governments.*
   ▸ *When the powers of the federal government and the powers of the state governments conflict, the federal government prevails.*

▸ *The necessary and proper clause, commerce clause, Civil Rights Act of 1964, categorical grants, and federal mandates have all increased the power of the federal government relative to the states.*

▸ *The procedure for amending the Constitution illustrates the federal structure of American government.*

▸ *Federalism decentralizes political conflict, provides interest groups with multiple points of access, and creates opportunities for experimentation and diversity of public policy.*

▸ *Federalism enables interest groups to delay or even thwart majority support for a policy.*

3. SELECTION OF SUPREME COURT JUSTICES

▸ *Supreme Court justices are appointed by the president and confirmed by a majority vote of the Senate.*

▸ *The process by which Supreme Court justices are nominated and confirmed illustrates the system of checks and balances.*

▸ *Presidents select Supreme Court justices who have impressive credentials and possess needed racial, ethnic, and gender characteristics.*

▸ *Presidents with a philosophy of judicial restraint look for candidates who use precedent and the Framers' original intent to decide cases.*

▸ *Presidents with a philosophy of judicial activism look for candidates who believe that the Supreme Court must correct injustices when other branches or the states fail to do so.*

4. THE ELECTORAL COLLEGE

▸ *The president and vice president are not elected by a direct vote of the people. Instead, the winning ticket must receive a majority of the votes in the electoral college.*

▸ *The electoral college is a winner-take-all system in which the candidate who wins a plurality of the votes in a state wins all of that state's electoral votes.*

▸ *The winner-take-all feature of the electoral college makes it difficult for third-party candidates to succeed.*

▸ *The electoral college system encourages presidential candidates to focus on campaigning in the most populous states.*

▸ *If none of the presidential candidates receives a majority of the electoral votes, the selection process moves to the House of Representatives, where each state has one vote.*

▸ *The electoral college benefits the small states.*

5. AFRICAN AMERICAN VOTING PATTERNS

▸ *African Americans have consistently supported Democratic presidential candidates since the New Deal.*

▸ *African Americans tend to support the more liberal candidates within the Democratic Party.*

▸ *Studies reveal that, when the effects of race and education are eliminated, African Americans have higher voting rates than do whites.*

6. VOTER TURNOUT

▸ *The voter turnout in the United States is lower than that of most Western democracies.*

▸ *The majority of the U.S. electorate does not vote in a nonpresidential election.*

▸ *People with more education are more likely to vote than people with less education.*

▸ *People with more income are more likely to vote than people with less income.*

▸ *Older people are more likely to vote than younger people.*

▸ *Women are more likely to vote than men.*

▸ *Cross-pressures, a low level of political efficacy, and voter registration are all factors that reduce voter turnout.*

7. DIVIDED GOVERNMENT

▸ *Divided government occurs when the presidency and Congress are controlled by different parties.*

▸ *Divided government heightens partisanship, slows the legislative process, and contributes to the decline in public trust in government.*

▸ *Presidents attempt to overcome the problems posed by divided government by using the media to generate public support, threatening to veto objectionable legislation, and building coalitions with key interest groups.*

8. POLITICAL ACTION COMMITTEES (PACs)

▸ *Business PACs have dramatically increased in number since the 1970s.*

▸ *PACs play a particularly significant role in supporting incumbent members of the House of Representatives.*

▸ *The amount of money that PACs can directly contribute to an individual candidate is limited by law.*

9. THE VETO POWER

▸ *The system of checks and balances gives the president the power to veto a bill and Congress the power to override a presidential veto.*

▸ *A pocket veto occurs when Congress adjourns within ten days of submitting a bill to the president. The president can let the bill die by neither signing it nor vetoing it.*

▸ *Presidents often use the threat of a veto to persuade Congress to modify a bill.*

▸ *Congress is usually unable to override a presidential veto.*

▸ *Most state governors can exercise a line-item veto.*

▸ *Congress passed the Line-Item Veto Act (1996) giving the president the power to veto individual items in major appropriations bills.*

▸ *In the case of* Clinton v. City of New York *(1998), the Supreme Court struck down the line-item veto as an unconstitutional violation of the principle of separation of powers.*

10. THE PRESIDENT AND THE CABINET

▸ *The president appoints cabinet heads subject to confirmation by the Senate. However, the president can fire a cabinet head without Senate approval.*

▸ *Cabinet members often have divided loyalties. Their loyalty to the president can be undermined by their loyalty to the institutional goals of their own department.*

▸ *Presidents often experience difficulty in controlling cabinet departments because they form iron triangles with interest groups and congressional committees.*

11. PRESIDENTIAL PRIMARIES

▸ *Presidential primaries have weakened party control over the nomination process.*

▸ *In a closed primary, voters are required to identify a party preference before the election and are not allowed to split their ticket.*

▸ *The Democratic Party now uses a proportional system that awards delegates based on the percentage of votes a candidate receives.*

▸ *Primary voters tend to be party activists who are older and more affluent than the general electorate.*

▸ *Frontloading is the recent pattern of states holding primaries in February and March to capitalize on media attention and to maximize their influence in the nomination process.*

12. STANDING COMMITTEES AND THE SENIORITY SYSTEM

▸ *Standing committees are permanent bodies that focus on legislation in a particular area. Thus, they promote specialized policy expertise among their members.*

▸ *All bills are referred to standing committees, where they can be amended, passed, or killed. Most bills are killed.*

▸ *Standing committees are divided into subcommittees, where the details of legislation are refined.*

▸ *In the past, committee chairs were chosen by a seniority system in which the majority party members with the most continuous service on the committee became the chair. Although chairs are now elected, most still tend to be senior members of the majority party.*

▸ *The system of standing committees is particularly important in the House of Representatives. The House Rules Committee plays a pivotal role. It places a bill on the legislative calendar, determines the type of amendment allowed, and allocates the time for debate.*

13. THE FEDERALIST PAPERS

▸ *In* Federalist *No. 10, Madison argued that political factions are undesirable but inevitable.*

▸ *Madison believed that the excesses of factionalism could be limited by the system of republican government created by the Constitution.*

▸ *Federalist No. 10 refuted the widely held belief that a republican form of government would work only in a small geographically compact territory. He argued that a large republic such as the United States would fragment political power and thus curb the threat posed by both majority and minority factions.*

14. THE FOURTEENTH AMENDMENT AND SELECTIVE INCORPORATION

▸ *The Fourteenth Amendment made African Americans citizens, thus voiding the* Dred Scott *decision.*

▸ *The Fourteenth Amendment's Due Process Clause forbids a state from acting in an unfair or arbitrary way. Its Equal Protection Clause forbids a state from discriminating against or drawing unreasonable distinctions between persons.*

▸ *The doctrine of selective incorporation uses the Fourteenth Amendment to extend most of the requirements of the Bill of Rights to the states.*

15. POLITICAL SOCIALIZATION

▸ *Political socialization is the process by which political values are formed and passed from one generation to the next.*

▸ *The family is the most important agent of political socialization. Parents usually pass their party identification to their children.*

16. CRITICAL ELECTION

▸ *A critical election takes place when groups of voters change their traditional patterns of party loyalty.*

▸ *Critical elections trigger a party realignment in which the minority party displaces the majority party, thus ushering in a new party era.*

▸ *The presidential elections of 1800, 1860, 1896, and 1932 were all critical elections that transformed U.S. politics.*

17. THE SELECTION OF SUPREME COURT CASES

▸ *Most of the cases on the Supreme Court's docket are derived from the High Court's appellate jurisdiction.*

▸ *Nearly all appellate cases now reach the Supreme Court by a writ of certiorari.*

▸ *According to the Rule of Four, at least four of the nine justices must agree to hear a case.*

▸ *The Supreme Court refuses to hear most of the lower court appeals.*

18. THE MASS MEDIA

▸ *The mass media play a key role in affecting which issues the public thinks are important. These issues usually reach the government's policy agenda.*

▸ *Horse-race journalism refers to the media's tendency to focus on polls, personalities, and sound bites rather than on in-depth analysis of key issues.*

19. THE ARTICLES OF CONFEDERATION

▸ *The Articles of Confederation established a decentralized system of government with a weak central government that had limited powers over the states.*

▸ *The Articles created a unicameral Congress that lacked the power to levy taxes or regulate interstate trade.*

20. THE ROLE OF STATE LEGISLATURES

▸ *In the original Constitution, state legislatures chose U.S. senators. As a result of the Seventeenth Amendment, senators are now elected by voters in each state.*

▸ *State legislatures have the power to determine the boundary lines of congressional districts.*

▸ *State legislatures can ratify constitutional amendments by a vote of three-fourths of the states.*

KEY THEMES AND FACTS

PART IV:

TEST-TAKING STRATEGIES

Strategies for the Multiple-Choice Questions

Your AP U.S. Government and Politics exam will begin with a 45-minute section containing 60 multiple-choice questions. Each multiple-choice question is worth 1 point. The 60 multiple-choice questions are worth a total of 60 points, or half of the 120 points that are on the exam. Recently, the College Board changed the scoring of the multiple-choice sections of AP exams. The score achieved on the multiple-choice section of the exam will be based on the number of questions answered correctly. Points will not be deducted for incorrect answers or unanswered questions.

With this change, the "guessing penalty" is eliminated, but don't waste precious time. If you do not have any idea how to answer a question, skip it and move on. If you can eliminate two or more answers, you should use the process of elimination to make an educated guess.

A GRAND STRATEGY

The multiple-choice questions are vital to achieving a high score. Although they account for just under one-third of the exam's total time, they are worth 50 percent of its total points. Never forget that you need only about 90 points to score a 5 and 75 points to score a 4.

The multiple-choice questions cover very predictable topics. About one-third of the questions will be devoted to Congress and the presidency. Another twelve to fifteen questions will cover key terms not covered in the Congress and presidency questions and landmark Supreme Court cases. In addition, most exams devote three to four questions to charts and one question to a political cartoon. These graphics questions are particularly straightforward because all of the information you need is provided in the chart or cartoon.

Chapters 2–19 in this book contain all of the information you will need to ace the multiple-choice questions. If you carefully review these chapters, you should be able to correctly answer at least 48 of the 60 multiple-choice questions. If you miss 8 questions and leave 4 blank, this will give you a raw score of 46 points. You will then need only another 44 points to score a 5 and just 29 points to score a 4!

THREE CHALLENGING FORMATS

Most AP U.S. Government and Politics multiple-choice questions are very straightforward. However, test writers do use three formats that require closer examination.

DEFINITIONAL QUESTIONS

Vocabulary plays a particularly important role on AP U.S. Government and Politics exams. Tests usually contain twelve to fifteen multiple-choice questions designed to test your knowledge of key terms. In one typical format, the question gives you the definition and asks you to find the correct term. A second format reverses this pattern by giving you the term and asking you to find the definition. And finally, test writers often use a third format asking you to find an example of a term. Here are examples of each of these three formats:

1. **Those who believe that the Supreme Court should use its rulings to correct social injustices advocate**

    (A) *strict scrutiny*

    (B) *selective incorporation*

    (C) *judicial restraint*

    (D) stare decisis

    (E) *judicial activism*

The correct answer is E. Answer choice A is incorrect because strict scrutiny is the Supreme Court rule that classification by race and ethnic background is inherently suspect. Answer choice B is incorrect because selective incorporation is the case-by-case process by which liberties listed in the Bill of Rights have been applied to the states using the Due Process Clause of the Fourteenth Amendment. Answer choice C is incorrect because judicial restraint is the philosophy that the Supreme Court should use precedent and the Framers' original intent to decide cases. And finally, answer choice D is incorrect because *stare decisis* means to decide a case based on precedent established in earlier cases.

2. **The term *unitary government* refers to a political system in which**

   (A) *power is divided between a central government and regional governments*

   (B) *a weak central government has limited power over the regional governments*

   (C) *all power is vested in a central government*

   (D) *power and responsibility are transferred from the national government to state and local governments*

   (E) *the national government grants funds to the states for broadly defined purposes*

The correct answer is C. Answer choice A is the definition of a federal system of government. Answer choice B is the definition of a confederate system of government. Answer choice D is the definition of devolution. And finally, answer choice E is the definition of a block grant.

3. **Which of the following is an example of monetary policy?**

   (A) *The Federal Reserve Board raises interest rates to control inflation.*

   (B) *The House Ways and Means Committee closes a loophole in the tax code.*

   (C) *The Office of Management and Budget cuts budget requests from federal agencies in order to reduce the budget deficit.*

   (D) *The Congressional Budget Office predicts that a health care proposal will cost more than expected.*

   (E) *The president pledges to balance the federal budget by the end of his or her term in office.*

The correct answer is A because monetary policy involves adjusting interest rates. Answer choices B, C, D, and E all illustrate fiscal policy because they involve raising or lower taxes and government spending programs.

"EXCEPT" QUESTIONS

Between three and five questions on each exam will provide you with four answers that are correct and one answer that is incorrect. Known as EXCEPT questions, these problems ask you to find the answer that does not fit or is incorrect. The best strategy is to treat these questions as if they were five-part true-false questions. Simply go through the question and label each answer choice "true" or "false." The correct answer is the one that is false. Here are three examples:

1. **All of the following are commonly used by interest groups to influence public policy EXCEPT**

    (A) *participating in iron triangles*

    (B) *paying for media campaigns*

    (C) *forming PACs*

    (D) *selecting candidates*

    (E) *endorsing candidates*

The correct answer is D. Answer choices A, B, C, and E are common strategies used by interest groups to influence public policy. However, unlike political parties, interest groups do not select candidates.

2. **All of the following limit the president's ability to influence domestic policymaking in Congress EXCEPT**

    (A) *mandatory spending on entitlement programs*

    (B) *party polarization*

    (C) *the lame-duck period*

    (D) *divided government*

    (E) *access to national news media*

The correct answer is E. Answer choices A, B, C, and D all limit the president's ability to influence domestic policymaking in Congress. However, the president's unparalleled access to the national news media enables him or her to influence public opinion and control the policy agenda.

3. **All of the following have been used to increase the power of the federal government relative to the states EXCEPT**

   (A) *federal mandates*

   (B) *block grants*

   (C) *categorical grants*

   (D) *the commerce clause*

   (E) *selective incorporation*

The correct answer is B. Answer choices A, C, D, and E all increase the power of the federal government relative to the states. However, block grants increase the power of the states because they do not come with specific federal requirements.

QUESTIONS ABOUT SUPREME COURT CASES

Supreme Court cases usually play a prominent role on AP U.S. Government and Politics exams. Tests typically contain three to five multiple-choice questions designed to test your knowledge of key cases and constitutional principles. In a typical format, the question gives you a case and asks for the ruling. A second format reverses this pattern by giving you the ruling and asking you to find the case. And finally, test writers sometimes use a third format in which they ask you to analyze a brief but noteworthy opinion from a famous case. Here are examples of each of these three formats:

1. **In *Griswold v. Connecticut*, the Supreme Court ruled that**

   (A) *there is a constitutional right to privacy*

   (B) *strict quota systems are illegal*

   (C) *the exclusionary rule applies to the states*

   (D) *the principle of "one person, one vote" can be applied to state legislative districts*

   (E) *the Bill of Rights cannot be applied to the states*

The correct answer is A. Answer choice B is from *Regents of the University of California v. Bakke*. Answer choice C is from *Mapp v. Ohio*. Answer choice D is from *Baker v. Carr*. And answer choice E is from *Barron v. Baltimore*.

2. **Which of the following Supreme Court cases struck down regulations limiting the amount of money individuals can contribute to their own campaign?**

   (A) Wesberry v. Sanders

   (B) Grutter v. Bollinger

   (C) Texas v. Johnson

   (D) Buckley v. Valeo

   (E) United States v. Nixon

The correct answer is D. Answer choice A established the principle of "one person, one vote" in drawing congressional districts. Answer choice B upheld the affirmative action policy of the University of Michigan Law School. Answer choice C ruled that flag burning is a form of symbolic speech protected by the First Amendment. And finally, answer choice E ruled that there is no constitutional guarantee of unqualified executive privilege.

3. **Question 3 is based on the following excerpt from a major Supreme Court decision:**

"It is no part of the business of government to compose official prayers for any group of American people to recite as part of a religious program carried on by government."

This decision of the Supreme Court upheld the principle that

   (A) *there are no limits to the free exercise of religious beliefs*

   (B) *free speech can be restricted when there is a "clear and present danger"*

   (C) *there is a "wall of separation" between church and state*

   (D) *symbolic speech can be protected by the First Amendment*

(E) *prior restraint is a violation of the First Amendment protection of a free press*

The correct answer is C. The excerpt is from the majority opinion in *Engel v. Vitale*. This landmark case struck down state-sponsored prayer in the public schools as an unconstitutional violation of the Establishment Clause.

Strategies for the Free-Response Questions

After completing the multiple-choice questions, you will receive a short break. You will then have 100 minutes to complete four free-response questions. Each question is worth a total of 15 points.

PRACTICE MATERIALS

Practice is key to performing well on the free-response questions. Although practice will not guarantee a perfect score, it will help you earn a high score. You should visit the AP U.S. Government and Politics Course homepage at AP Central (*www.apcentral. collegeboard.org*). There you will find a full set of free-response questions and sample essays from 1999 to the present.

STRATEGIES FOR SUCCESS

Using authentic practice materials is important. Following good test-taking strategies is essential. This section will discuss six strategies that will help you achieve high scores on your free-response questions.

1. WATCH YOUR TIME

The free-response section is like a four-part sprint. You must be focused and ready to "hit the ground running" on each question. Remember, you have only 25 minutes for each question. If you have written an SAT or ACT essay, you should have a good sense of how much you can write in 25 minutes. Do not spend too much time on a single question or on part of a question. As you complete your answers, look at the classroom clock to make sure you are leaving enough time for each question.

2. WRITE DIRECT ANSWERS FOR FOCUSED, MULTIPART QUESTIONS

Students who prepare for the AP United States History, AP European History, and AP World History exams are taught to prepare for questions that require a thesis statement, supporting evidence, and a conclusion. The AP U.S. Government and Politics free-response questions use very focused, multipart questions that do not require the traditional thesis-driven format. Your task is to clearly and directly answer each part of the question.

3. BE PREPARED TO DEFINE KEY CONCEPTS

Many questions include parts that ask you to define key terms. For example, recent exams asked students to define *policy agenda*, *congressional redistricting*, *fiscal policy*, and *monetary policy*. Chapter 2 provides a list of key terms that you need to know for both the multiple-choice questions and the free-response questions.

4. BE PREPARED TO LIST, DESCRIBE, DISCUSS, AND EXPLAIN

Every question includes a part asking you to list, describe, discuss, or explain a concept, political process, governmental institution, or constitutional principle. Carefully read each question to make sure that you understand what it is asking you to do. If you are asked to write an explanation, try to include a "for example" sentence to illustrate your point. For example, you could note that the 2000 presidential election illustrates how the electoral college limits majority rule. Although Al Gore received more popular votes than George W. Bush, he received fewer electoral votes and thus lost the election.

5. ADD A SPARE TIRE

Many questions specifically ask you to discuss "two different ways," "two reasons why," or "two factors that." For example, a recent question asked students to "explain two reasons why the electoral college has not been abolished." Although you must provide the required two reasons to receive full credit, you can add a third ("spare tire") reason. Your "spare tire" reason will not count against you. AP readers are required to read all three reasons and give you credit for the best two. Unfortunately, you cannot earn extra points.

6. MAKE STUDYING CONGRESS AND THE PRESIDENCY A PRIORITY

The AP U.S. Government and Politics Development Committee works very hard to write a variety of free-response questions that cover key topics from the Course Description curriculum outline. Trying to guess which question will be asked is usually futile. However, we can say that every exam since 1999 has included at least one free-response question on Congress and/or the presidency. As you prepare for the exam, be sure to carefully review these all-important topics.

Notes

Notes

Notes

Notes

Notes

Notes